I0150003

# Living a Fake Life for a Real God?

## Seeking God's Imprint for an Authentic Life

Shaniqua Rischer

Copyright © 2013 by Shaniqua Rischer
All rights reserved. Except as permitted under the U.S. Copyright Act of
1976, no part of this publication may be reproduced, distributed, or
transmitted in any form or by any means, or stored in a database or
retrieval system, without the prior written permission of the publisher.

Unless otherwise indicated, Scriptures noted NLT are taken from the
New Living Translation Bible

Scriptures noted KJV are taken from the King James Version of the Bible.

Scripture taken from the New King James Version®. Copyright © 1982
by Thomas Nelson, Inc. Used by permission. All rights reserved

.

Scriptures noted ESV are taken from the English Standard Version of the
Bible.

Scriptures noted CEB are taken from the Contemporary English Bible.

Scriptures noted CEV are taken from the Contemporary English Version
of the Bible.

Scriptures noted NIV are taken from the New International Version of
the Bible.

Scriptures noted NASB are taken from the New American Standard Bible.

Scriptures noted NIRV are taken from the New International Reader's
Version of the Bible.

Scriptures noted "The Message" are taken from The Messages. Copyright
© 1993, 1994, 1995, 1996, 2000, 2001, 2002, Used by permission of
NavPress Publishing Group.

All rights reserved.

ISBN: 0615865860
ISBN-13: 978-0615865867

# DEDICATION

To my nephews (Ashton, Aidan, and Gilford)…my honeys…
May your journey with Him be full of grace, mercy, and most
of all favor

&

To those who hunger for more…

*"Since you have heard about Jesus and have learned the truth
that comes from him, throw off your old sinful nature and your
former way of life, which is corrupted by lust and deception.
Instead, let the Spirit renew your thoughts and attitudes. Put on
your new nature, created to be like God—truly righteous and
holy." Ephesians 4:21-24 NLT*

# CONTENTS

# Acknowledgements

*In church, before a guest preacher gets up to preach they always start their acknowledgements with the same five words… "Giving all honor to God". Even though this is not a sermon, I would be remiss to start with anything less than that. First, giving all honor to God, my Lord and Savior, Jesus Christ. I am nothing without you and I thank you for showing me how to live life more authentically and abundantly.*

*To my parents, there are no amount of words that can convey the depth of my love for you. You have supported me through the highs, lows and all the dreams in between. Thank you.*

*To my siblings, Roderick and Demetra, and my extended family, I can only do what I have done because you each have cheered me on in big and small ways. I will never forget everything you've done to keep me going. You guys **always** take care of me.*

*To Tamara, thank you for being my accountability partner through the years and thank you for the sacrifice you and Jonathan have made to sew into my ministry and the vision God gave me.*

*To Kacey, thank you for encouraging me and showing me there is another way to see your dreams come to fruition. Without you holding me accountable, this would still be an incomplete project.*

*To Jennifer Thompson, I didn't forget you! Thank you for your sacrifice in editing with this labor of love. I pray God blesses you abundantly for what you did for His ministry and one of His children.*

*To Andrea, Akilah, Brandie, Chenay (my besty), Cheryl (my sister-in-love), Christina, Delores, Erika, Kerri, Marci, Margo, Nissa, Tuvessia, and Seidra…thank you each for being my friend and my blessing. You each directly contributed to this book and ministry in ways you will never know (and some you do).*

*To The E-mail Crew…these all started with you. It's too many of y'all to name individually, but please know I am talking about each of you. I wrote my first devotional and shared it with you guys and didn't stop. You all, more than anyone, know how wordy I can be and were nice enough to read most of the what I wrote. LOL! Thank you for all of the discussions and memorable times to which there have been many.*

*And to all those not named, thank you. This is only the beginning so look for your name in the next book! Much love to each of you and walk with Him always.*

# Chapter 1: Intro - The Eldest Son...
# My Story

*"Jesus continued: "There was a man who had two sons. The younger one said to his father, "Father, give me my share of the estate." So he divided his property between them. "Not long after that, the younger son got together all he had, set off for a distant country and there squandered his wealth in wild living. After he had spent everything, there was a severe famine in that whole country, and he began to be in need. So he went and hired himself out to a citizen of that country, who sent him to his fields to feed pigs. He longed to fill his stomach with the pods that the pigs were eating, but no one gave him anything. "When he came to his senses, he said, "How many of my father's hired servants have food to spare, and here I am starving to death! I will set out and go back to my father and say to him: Father, I have sinned against heaven and against you. I am no longer worthy to be called your son; make me like one of your hired servants." So he got up and went to his father. "But while he was still a long way off, his father saw him and was filled with compassion for him; he ran to his son, threw his arms around him and kissed him. "The son said to him, "Father, I have sinned against heaven and against you. I am no longer worthy to be called your son." "But the father said to his servants, "Quick! Bring the best robe and put it on him. Put a ring on his finger and sandals on his feet. Bring the fattened calf and kill it. Let's have a feast and celebrate. For this son of mine was dead and is alive again; he was lost and is found." So they began to celebrate. "Meanwhile, the older son was in the field. When he came near the house, he heard music and dancing. So he called one of the servants and asked him what was going on. "Your brother has come,' he replied, 'and your father has killed the fattened calf because he has him back safe and sound." "The older brother became angry and refused to go in. So his father went out and pleaded with him. But he answered his father, "Look! All these years I've been slaving for you and never disobeyed your orders. Yet you never gave me even a young goat so I could celebrate with my friends. But when this son of yours who has squandered your property with prostitutes comes home,*

*you kill the fattened calf for him!" "My son," the father said, "you are always with me, and everything I have is yours. But we had to celebrate and be glad, because this brother of yours was dead and is alive again; he was lost and is found."" Luke 15:11-32 NIV*

There were seven of us sitting around the table at the hotel restaurant on the patio that morning. Before us was a scene of great beauty and tranquility as we looked at the coast and the Atlantic Ocean. It was a beautiful morning in The Gambia, yet as we all sat around for our morning devotional, I didn't expect to do this one thing especially in front of others. I cried.

I was on a mission trip with my church and my Pastor had assigned each of us to lead a devotional from the book, "Fully Devoted: Living Each Day in Jesus' Name". On this morning, one of our team members was leading a devotion based on the "Prodigal Son". It was a message I had heard many times before and honestly, I didn't expect to get that much more out of it. Although I had reviewed the lesson that morning, I still didn't see any correlation between the message and my life. Yet the more she talked and the more we reviewed the message in depth, the more broken I became. The tears started to flow. I could feel the glances of the others looking at me as the silent tears fell, but I was determined to believe that my shades would hide my bleeding heart.

Yet when it came time to share what we learned, I opened up and shared my story. I wasn't the "Prodigal Son". I was much worse. I was the elder son. I carried bitterness towards my Father, a deep bitterness that even I had not recognized until that moment. In my heart, I was angry with God. I felt disappointed. I felt betrayed. I was the eldest son; I stayed home, I stayed close to the Father, not venturing too far from Him, always trying to obey and not live a life unpleasing to Him. Yes, I was frustrated at obeying Him at times, of not experiencing life like others, but I had my duties. Not always accepting them with a glad heart, I accepted my duties. All the while bitterness seeped into my heart. Bitterness that showed itself when one of my close friends, unmarried, had become pregnant. She wasn't the first friend I had that was to become pregnant outside of marriage. We are all in our mid 30s and in this day and age, it's more of a norm than not to be unmarried and expecting; this is now acceptable. We are all beyond the age of accountability and responsibility. Although I never held any bitterness towards her and her boyfriend as both of them are my friends and I rejoiced in their blessing, I had bitterness towards God. Because in their sin, which is what it clearly was on many levels, God blessed them with something I am not sure I will ever have. That is a child of my own. I am not sleeping with random people or wanting to trap someone in order to become pregnant. As a matter of fact, at the age of 35, I am still a virgin. Still waiting and attempting to be patient. I must admit that I am almost hypersensitive of my witness and confession because I don't want to cause anyone to question Christ by looking at my life. Believe me, I've seen more than my share of Christian hypocrites. Therefore, the older I get, the more I have ceased doing a lot of things because I desire to live a life that pleases God and not me. Yet, as I have been dutiful, my resentment grew again and it wasn't until I was shown my heart that I had to repent for my heart. How do you look at your Father and serve Him, knowing that everywhere around you others are being blessed in their sinful living? This newly created life, a child, is a blessing. Not having a disease and you have lived sexually promiscuous (male or female) is a blessing. Abandoning a child out of wedlock and years later that child welcomes you in their life is a blessing. Having an abortion, but still having the ability to conceive and have children is a blessing. Being a cheater, but still finding someone to love you in spite of your past is a blessing. Having a one night stand and being able to walk away with only a memory and no harm is a blessing. All around ME, I have seen blessing after blessing in many of my friend's sinful living. How do you reconcile that?

You have no idea of how that broke me to admit to myself and others because I love my Father, Abba. I love God, but I wondered, "Why me?" and "Why not me?" Since then, He hasn't answered my desire for a mate and a family, but He has provided a balm for a wound I ignored. Now, as the "eldest" daughter, I realize that my friend may have the blessing of a beautiful son and I would never begrudge her that joy; but neither do I want her journey. It has not been easy. The lesson I learned had nothing to do with her or any of my other friends, but everything to do with me and my Father.

The eldest son in this parable never fully recognized the love and access that he ALWAYS had with the Father. He didn't have to come back broken and humble like his brother and he didn't have to experience hurt, hunger, and being treated less than a prince. He didn't have to accept half of anything because he always had everything. Instead, he was always known as the

Father's inheritor and was respected as such. I've known heartache, but I haven't known heartache on the level of pieces of my soul being left with different people from sharing myself sexually with them. I haven't always accepted it, but I know I am the daughter of the Most High God, a princess. I now accept nothing less than my due as His daughter. I don't have to deal with lifelong consequences from choices made outside of God's will with regards to sex and broken relationships. Many that I know do and may have to in the future. I bask in His presence daily and ALL that He has is for me. He has never been unaware of my dedication and sacrifice, even while He knew my resentful heart. He has always sent me love letters that before I never noticed because my heart wasn't ready to receive them. Now they are.

As I grow closer to God, He continues to reveal aspects of me that I do not want to acknowledge because it will mean I am not nearly as "good" as I would like to believe. At the same time, as I get closer to God, He reveals just how much He does cherish me because of my obedience and my faithfulness and just how much favor I am given. Favor isn't fair, but it is a reward. I am thankful for both revelations as both are me.

If you are the "Prodigal Son" or the eldest son, you are still His child. He loves you and nothing can separate us from that love. "For I am sure that neither death nor life, nor angels nor rulers, nor things present nor things to come, nor powers, nor height nor depth, nor anything else in all creation, will be able to separate us from the love of God in Christ Jesus our Lord." (Romans 8:38-39 NIV).

May you read these devotions from my journey and discover what it means to have a truly authentic life for a real God.

# Chapter 2: Rebirth - Moment of Great Despair

### A Moment of Great Despair

*"The Lord is my shepherd, I lack nothing. He makes me lie down in green pastures, He leads me beside quiet waters, He refreshes my soul. He guides me along the right paths for His name's sake. Even though I walk through the darkest valley, I will fear no evil, for You are with me; Your rod and Your staff, they comfort me. You prepare a table before me in the presence of my enemies. You anoint my head with oil; my cup overflows. Surely Your goodness and love will follow me all the days of my life, and I will dwell in the house of the Lord forever." Psalm 23 NIV*

Yesterday, someone I care for lost his younger brother. He suffered a stroke last week. He was only in his twenties. Yesterday, I also spoke with a friend whose young cousin, barely a teenager, was beat in a crack house. It is unclear why she was there, but it is apparent that her mother knew that she was there. Last Friday, I woke up with a terrible pain in my eye. After going to the doctor, I learned that somehow I had a corneal ulcer and without aggressive medication and treatment, I could lose the sight in my left eye in a matter of weeks. Within the past week, I have been to the doctor three times for follow up care - I am hoping for the best, in spite of today, feeling the worse.

While doing my graduate coursework at DBU, I wrote a paper in my theology class. Although I don't remember the title, it questioned the purpose of pain and suffering from a just God. Despite how well written the paper, I received a B+. My professor said I failed to give enough scriptural support. Perhaps, although I had experienced my fair share of the former, I hadn't grasped enough understanding of the later to support why pain existed-scripturally or not.

There is a room in my house that I have the following words painted on an entire wall. It is pretty magnificent to behold, but for me, it makes me pause every day.

**For I know the plans I have for you," declares the LORD.**

**Jeremiah 29:11 NIV**

As I cried, I had to ask "Do you God?" Was it your plan for a young man to die before his time? Was it your plan for your young daughter to be beat in a crack house? One more injustice this young life had to endure. Is it your plan for me to lose sight? Is it punishment for the words I spoke last week when I simply refused to do your ministry because the cost was too much for me? He answered me, "Trust Me." Simply, trust Him.

No words I can ever speak will give comfort to a family who has lost a son, brother, or child. No words I can ever speak will help my friend make peace with the destruction that is going on within her family. However, the words I tell myself give me comfort. Trust Him. Do you know why? Scripture played a part (I can quote scripture), yet my relationship is the key. In my moments of greatest despair, I have met the Lord Jesus for myself. It is in the moments of great despair, that you too, will meet Him. You will only trust someone whose love you have felt in your deepest spirit. You will only learn to trust someone whose character you know. Jehovah- Shammah, the Lord is there. El-Shaddai, the Lord is Sufficient. Jehovah – Shalom, the Lord is Peace. So many names, so many ways to know Him, and so many ways to experience trusting Him.

My testimony is just that, mine. God has called you to your own. And as I think about what scripture can possibly sum all of that up, I think of the 23rd Psalm. It is more than David's testimony, it is my testimony, it is your testimony, and quite simply it is God telling you to trust Him.

Shaniqua Rischer

"The LORD is my shepherd; I shall not be in want.  He makes me lie down in green pastures, he leads me beside quiet waters, he restores my soul. He guides me in paths of righteousness for his name's sake.  Even though I walk through the valley of the shadow of death, I will fear no evil, for you are with me; your rod and your staff, they comfort me.  You prepare a table before me in the presence of my enemies.  You anoint my head with oil; my cup overflows.  Surely goodness and love will follow me all the days of my life, and I will dwell in the house of the LORD forever."

*Prayer: Lord, you are the Lord of all, Ruler of all men, and Creator of all nations.  So often, we don't fully understand what it means to trust you until we are confronted with death, sickness, or hurt.  Yet we do know that in all things you are sovereign.  We will never understand some parts of our journey and neither me, nor any theologian will ever be able to explain the reason of "why", but as we lift our eyes towards you we remain comforted in the fact that you have not nor ever will forsake us. Today, tomorrow, always. Amen.*

**Reflection & Study Questions**

**1. Have you ever felt despair and separated from God?**

**2. What have your moments of great despair taught you about God?**

# Change

*"If a man dies, shall he live again? All the days of my appointed time will I wait, till my change come. Thou shalt call, and I will answer thee: thou wilt have a desire to the work of thine hands. For now thou numberest my steps: dost thou not watch over my sin?" Job 14:14-16 KJV*

I never would have thought I would love the King James Version of the Bible, but I do. After struggling with understanding it for so many years and preferring the Contemporary English Version, I now have grown to love and appreciate the symmetry of words that are used. This verse is a perfect example of that. The other versions didn't speak to me, like this version did. As I read it, I remembered the phase of life I inhabit now, which is one that most people (myself included) would prefer not to occur. That phase of life is change. Now, regardless if you say you embrace change, we all struggle with it because although inevitable, it is unknown. And we, as humans, don't like not knowing and therefore we often have issues embracing change.

The thing about this verse that struck me was that Job was prepared to wait for that change. What happens in your life that makes you want to have change? Usually, it is as you are going through a painful period of time or when you feel you have reached the pinnacle of some goal; looking for the next new horizon to be conquered. In this instance, Job has encountered a painful period of his life. He has lost everything. His family, wealth, health, and now it looks as if he is losing his friends. But what he hasn't lost is God. And not losing God means all Job has to do is wait on God. And waiting on God is hard to do. I'll be the first to admit it. Extremely hard, especially when you feel as if your back is up against a wall and you do not see any way out. This is where we meet Job. He has nowhere to go, but up and up doesn't look promising to him. So, what does it mean to wait on God?

It means to trust Him in your situation. There is a difference between faith and trust. Verse 15 states that God will call our names and we will answer Him. Well, what if we don't want to answer? Sometimes, God will call us where we are afraid of going…a relationship, a new job, a new house, etc. What if our trust in God is shaky? Although God has proven Himself to each of us time and again, we often forget what that means. What if God calls us to leave the situation we are in to do something else? Maryanne

Williamson said "Our deepest fear is not that we are inadequate. Our deepest fear is that we are powerful beyond measure". When God calls you to another place, an unknown place, it takes trust. Verse 16 speaks to God walking our journey with us. He hasn't forsaken us. When we can't see Him or hear Him that does not mean we are walking alone. Even when we stray away from Him, God is waiting on us to come back to him. And that is what waiting on God is all about; trusting Him to lead you in your journey back to Him. When you wait for your change, you are showing God mustard seed faith. You are waiting for your situation to change and more importantly, you are trusting God with control of your life to take you to the next level. The unknown. Sometimes that path is circular, straight, or a detour. But it's a path you have to walk all the same. Although freely admitting He was waiting on God, this is a point where Job was struggling. God still had not answered the soon to be asked question of "why". In fact, God doesn't answer most of Jobs questions, ever. Instead, he reminds Job to know that He is God and that He is the giver of blessings and life.

So, if your back is up against a wall and you don't see the end near, step out on faith and trust God to number your steps, respond to His call as He guides you to the next level, and more than anything wait until He says it's time to move. It will come. Eventually, God will tell you to move and that the wait is over. So, as you wait, use that time as a time of preparation. Because when you walk into "change", by sheer principle alone, you can't walk out of it the same person as before.

**Reflection & Study Questions**

**1. How do you deal with change?**

**2. Where do you feel God is calling you to change in your life?**

**3. Identify areas in your life that need to change.**

# Trust Him

*"And rend your heart, and not your garments, and turn unto the LORD your God: for he is gracious and merciful, slow to anger, and of great kindness, and repenteth him of the evil." Joel 2:13 NKJV*

*"The LORD also shall roar out of Zion, and utter his voice from Jerusalem; and the Heavens and the earth shall shake: but the LORD will be the hope of his people, and the strength of the children of Israel." Joel 3:16 NKJV*

The month of May was supposed to be a happy month for me. Out of all of the months this year, I expected that one month to be, if not great, good. It wasn't. Instead, I spent about 3.5 weeks out of 5, crying; some days and nights, back to back. And if you don't know...I hate crying. It's not something I do. I don't cry when I am hurt, emotionally or physically. I only cry when my soul and spirit have been cut and even then, I try to hide it. I lost something I cherished in May. The devil hit me in a place I thought I had mended years before, a long time ago. The devil is so sneaky and instead of coming at me face forward, he attacked me from the rear. As I near graduation, he has tried to break me on so many levels (because if God uses me to help one person form a relationship with Him, then that is victory).

This last month, I questioned my calling to minister to others. I questioned if I heard God speak to me in 2003 when I started school. I felt that I was empty and had given my all to everyone and everything else. Although I was being filled from various places, I wasn't being filled up. I was always pouring it out to other people, things, and situations. (I am not the only one, so who else has felt that?) But through it all, God remained faithful to me, because it was a struggle to remain faithful to Him. He kept whispering to me. He kept holding me.

The very place someone tore me down in is the very place God sent a new someone to build me back up. So, as I was reading Joel, it struck me (once again) that God will allow circumstances to break your heart/spirit, so that He can replace what is torn, with the mending of His grace, mercy, and love. All the things God did for me, He will and wants to do for you.

Someone knows what I am talking about. You too have been there or are

17

currently there. God is asking you to turn to Him. He will be your strength when you don't have any. He has you. You think your momma got you, or your daddy can save you, or your friends will be there in your time of need. They won't, not because they don't care or won't try, but because they are only human. God never fails. He never lets you down. God has many names all through how He has revealed Himself to us. He is our Rock (Zur), He is our shield (Magen), He is with us (Jehovah-Shammah), He heals, (Jehovah-Rophe), He is our Lord and Savior (Jesus Christ). So from these two verses of Joel, we learn something else about God. Our hearts/minds/spirits/souls will be broken, but God wants us to turn to Him during those times, to trust Him. And when the "lion" roars and the foundation of your "world" is shaken, He will continue to be a refuge for you. He will hold you up, when you don't think you can face another battle.

**Reflection & Study Questions**

**1. Where are you struggling to trust God?**

# An Oracle Is Within My Heart

*"An oracle is within my heart concerning the sinfulness of the wicked: There is no fear of God before his eyes. For in his own eyes he flatters himself too much to detect or hate his sin. The words of his mouth are wicked and deceitful; he has ceased to be wise and to do good. Even on his bed he plots evil; he commits himself to a sinful course and does not reject what is wrong. Your love, O LORD, reaches to the Heavens, your faithfulness to the skies. Your righteousness is like the mighty mountains, your justice like the great deep. O LORD, you preserve both man and beast. How priceless is your unfailing love! Both high and low among men find refuge in the shadow of your wings. They feast on the abundance of your house; you give them drink from your river of delights. For with you is the fountain of life; in your light we see light. Continue your love to those who know you, your righteousness to the upright in heart." Psalm 36:1-10 NIV*

An oracle is within my heart. What an interesting thing for David to say as he begins this Psalm. I knew what I defined "oracle" as, but I went to my handy desk Webster for the technical definition. An oracle is "person who delivers authoritative, wise, or highly regarded and influential pronouncements; a divine communication or revelation; any person or thing serving as an agency of divine communication." We would think that an oracle would be a person to deliver a message to us, but in verse 1, David has said an oracle is speaking directly to his heart. Instead of a person or thing, it is God that is speaking to David. He is speaking to the man David is and He is speaking on the House of Israel. And my, what things God says.

In verses 1 & 2, God gets to the heart of the matter: there is no fear of Him and man thinks so much of himself, that he no longer recognizes sin. When was the last time you really feared God? Or better yet, what you did yesterday, last night, or anticipate doing today, do you really recognize the wrong in it? And if you do, will that stop you? Did it stop me?

In verses 3 & 4, we see that we have forgotten what the phrase "speak no evil, hear no evil" means. We gossip, we use profane words, we view and read things that are not pleasing in the eyes of God. Even watching the news can bring us desensitization to the very things our heart should cry out against. Man is on such a sinful course, we no longer even bother to object to the wrongs that are prevalent. Not enough to enforce change. When was the last time, WE ever did something or protested something that brought about

19

change?

But in verse 5, we see a shift in the Psalm, that talks about the love and righteousness of God. How in God, refuge can be found by all of us.

Today, God is speaking to your heart. That small voice you hear, that whisper that directs you to do better, do right, is God. Don't fail to heed it. God was speaking to David personally, opening David's eyes to his own shortcomings, as well as his fellow man. But he also gave David the solution: following God. As you begin today, submit your day to God. Follow wherever He leads you. Be the witness that is needed today. He has called each of us to a purpose and that purpose begins anew, today. It is never too late to turn to Him and seek the refuge only He can give you.

**Reflection & Study Questions**

**There is an oracle within my heart and He is speaking to each of us.**

**1. What is the "oracle" speaking to you?**

**2. Are you listening and responding in faith?**

# I Will Praise the Lord

*"I will bless the LORD at all times; His praise shall continually be in my mouth. My soul shall make her boast in the LORD; the humble shall hear thereof and be glad. O magnify the LORD with me, and let us exalt His name together. I sought the LORD, and He heard me, and delivered me from all my fears. They looked unto Him and were lightened, and their faces were not ashamed. This poor man cried, and the LORD heard him, and saved him out of all his troubles. The angel of the LORD encampeth round about them that fear Him, and delivereth them. O taste and see that the LORD is good; blessed is the man that trusteth in Him! The LORD redeemeth the soul of His servants, and none of them that trust in Him shall be desolate." Psalm 34:1-8, 22 NIV*

Last night I sent a text to some friends asking to pray for my family. This morning, I found out the text didn't go through. By the time I got to resend it to them, it was too late. Out of all the prayers I have requested for me, my family, and others that God answered, it would be so easy for me to believe that one went unheard. That God just didn't get those fevered prayers. I told a friend yesterday, that in grief and mourning it is a simple touch that can ease pain, I knew it before and I learned it again today. And as I type this, I have so much sorrow in my heart. There is so much that I would love to tell God I am tired of, but I can't. I have a devotional to write. And that is good, because no matter what, I told Him long ago, wherever He leads me I would follow. I have crawled, stumbled, and fallen many times, but I haven't stopped following Him (and devil, I won't stop now). And this Psalm is another reason why I haven't.

Verse 1: "I will praise the Lord at all times..." Even as I am hurting, I have to praise. No matter the hurt, the silences that surround me, I have to praise God. And I am forced to ask why? The answer is because...because He is good, He is merciful, He didn't have to do what He did, because what adversity doesn't kill us, makes us stronger, because He loved us enough...to send His son to die for us. David was right, in the midst of hurt I will praise the Lord AT ALL TIMES.

Verse 8: "Oh taste and see that the Lord is good." That is the craziest thing David could have said, in my opinion. At least at first I looked at it that way. But then, God spoke to me. His glory, His magnificence, His being is an experience of the senses. We see God every day, His hand is not invisible. I taste God every day. I smell God every day. He is in every breath I take and everything I do. God has never left us because He is in us. We just have to see and know and understand.

Verse 22: None of them that trust in Him shall be desolate. I have found out that even in our greatest pain or fear, we are never alone. We may sometime think we are, but we aren't. God has put people in our lives to see us through, but more importantly He is there. The Holy Spirit comforts us, Jesus stands before us and the everlasting arm of God holds us. So, praise Him no matter what.

## Reflection & Study Questions

**1. Are you ready experience what it means to walk with God and know that you are never alone? Why or Why not?**

**2. What may be hindering you from committing to God?**

# Redeemer and Deliverer

*"Contend, O LORD, with those who contend with me; fight against those who fight against me. Take up shield and buckler; arise and come to my aid. Brandish spear and javelin against those who pursue me. Say to my soul, "I am your salvation." May those who seek my life be disgraced and put to shame; may those who plot my ruin be turned back in dismay. May those who delight in my vindication shout for joy and gladness; may they always say, "The LORD be exalted, who delights in the well-being of his servant." My tongue will speak of your righteousness and of your praises all day long." Psalm 35:1-4, 27-28 NIV*

As we near the conclusion of the first book of Psalms, David has made it clear that he has lived a life of strife, filled with enemies, disappointments, hurts, and hindrances. Yet through all of that, he has never stopped praising. His praise is a testament to the man he was and how he viewed God. And in verse 3, as he is speaking of who God is and what God will do, David ascribes very profound words to God. "I AM your salvation." Looking in the dictionary, "salvation" has two basic meanings. 1) To save, protect from harm, risk, or loss. Deliverance. 2) From a theological standpoint, deliverance from the power and penalty of sin. Redemption.

David begins his psalm speaking on God's salvation for him. He was speaking in both terms. Because David had seen God work miracles and wonders in his life before, he knew that God would protect him. He also knew God as being the most High God. Holy, Holy, Holy! Therefore, He knew with atonement, God would keep him from the penalty of sin. God would redeem him and his many mistakes. But it doesn't stop there. David used the name of God "I AM" to describe what God would do. I AM is a sacred name of God, but the reason why it is so unique is because the verb "am" is the same as "be". God was in David's past, He was in David's present, and He will be in David's future.

That is the same for all of us who know Him. Coming full circle 28 generations later (Matt 1:17), out of the House of David, Jesus Christ would come. Jesus, meaning "God is Salvation", and Christ being "the Anointed One".

Shaniqua Rischer

What God has done for David yesterday, He has done for you today. Every day, as you encounter the trials and tribulations of life, as well as the joyful moments that keep all of us going, God speaks to those that know Him. He says "I am your salvation". Deliverer and Redeemer. Do you believe that He and will do it for you?

**Reflection & Study Questions**

**1. Do you believe that God is your Deliver and Redeemer?**

**2. What has God delivered you from?**

**3. Where do you still struggle and feel God has remained silent? Do you trust Him to show up?**

# Wait Patiently On the Lord

*"I waited patiently for the LORD; he turned to me and heard my cry. He lifted me out of the slimy pit, out of the mud and mire; he set my feet on a rock and gave me a firm place to stand. He put a new song in my mouth, a hymn of praise to our God. Many will see and fear and put their trust in the LORD. I proclaim righteousness in the great assembly; I do not seal my lips, as you know, O LORD. I do not hide your righteousness in my heart; I speak of your faithfulness and salvation. I do not conceal your love and your truth from the great assembly. Do not withhold your mercy from me, O LORD; may your love and your truth always protect me. For troubles without number surround me; my sins have overtaken me, and I cannot see. They are more than the hairs of my head, and my heart fails within me." Psalm 40:1-3, 9-12 NIV*

It is 6:00 am, Saturday morning, and I had been up almost 2 hours. Because I had a night of regrets, the first thing that was on my mind was God and forgiveness. I struggled with forgiving myself for the same exact stumbling blocks that always seem to trip me up. And the more I stumble, the harder it is for me to ask for forgiveness. Not because I have accepted my wrong doings as the "norm", but because it is one more time I have to come to God being broken and in shame. Yet do you know the root cause of my stumbling, for not all, but some of my struggles? It is patience or the lack thereof.

In the very first verse, David addressed what many struggle with, the ability to wait on the Lord. So many times, we step outside of His will, only to find ourselves in a "slimy pit" (v. 2) or on a slippery slope. Doing what we said we wouldn't do or doing what we thought was best, because we lacked the patience to wait on God to perform His will. But what is interesting about this Psalm, is that it starts off with David acknowledging how God turned to him and heard his cry. David begins this psalm in reflection. He doesn't state how long he waited, but instead addresses how God acknowledged his cry/prayers. Through the process of waiting, God blessed David and all those around him. In verses 7 and 8, David had begun to understand what it meant to operate in God's will. To want what God wanted for his life, because he was aware that it was greater than even he, King David, could imagine. But it is verse 9 and 10, where we come to understand the point of waiting. From wherever David had come, he was a better person because God made him wait. David proclaimed the goodness of God because of waiting. David was able to speak on the faithfulness of God (which is astounding-we often think about our faith, but do you realize GOD IS FAITHFUL TO YOU?????), because God had sustained him during those hard times. David was able to tell others, bear witness because He waited on God. He was able to do all of that because, he waited.

God does not bless us solely because of "us"; He blesses us so that we may in turn bless others. So, no, you may not receive that promotion, when you want it. You may not get to go on the trip you planned. You may not be able to do or receive. But trust God, through the process. Believe He has heard your cries, listened to your prayers, and felt the groaning of your spirit. As He is perfecting you in His will, understand there is a blessing for you and for others, in simply waiting.

**Reflection & Study Questions**

**1. How many blessings have you missed, because you failed to recognize God was deliberately having you to wait?**

**2. What lessons have you learned from being patient?**

# God Is In Control/ Trust in God's Love

*"You people may be strong and brag about your sins, but God can be trusted day after day. You plan brutal crimes, and your lying words cut like a sharp razor. You would rather do evil than good, and tell lies than speak the truth. You love to say cruel things, and your words are a trap. God will destroy you forever! He will grab you and drag you from your homes. You will be uprooted and left to die. When good people see this fearsome sight, they will laugh and say, "Just look at them now! Instead of trusting God, they trusted their wealth and their cruelty." But I am like an olive tree growing in God's house, and I can count on his love forever and ever. I will always thank God for what he has done; I will praise his good name when his people meet". Psalm 52 CEV*

*"Why do you take pride in wrong-doing, O powerful man? The loving-kindness of God lasts all day long. Your tongue makes plans to destroy like a sharp knife, you who lie. You love what is bad more than what is good, and you speak lies more than you speak the truth. You love all words that destroy, O lying tongue. But God will destroy you forever. He will pick you up and pull you away from your tent. He will pull up your roots from the land of the living. And those who are right will see and be afraid. They will laugh at him, saying, "Look, the man who would not make God his safe place, but trusted in his many riches and was strong in his sinful desire." But I am like a green olive tree in the house of God. I trust in the loving kindness of God forever and ever. I will give You thanks forever because of what You have done. And I will hope in Your name, for it is good to be where those who belong to You are." Psalm 52 NKJV*

For this devotional, I thought it best to use two different translations of the text. One translation sums this psalm up as "God is in control", the other "Trust in God's love". Both are correct, but each can be read decidedly different because the psalm is broken into two different sections.

How many times have you told your friends about the dirt you did? Did you brag about? Well, maybe not brag...but you definitely let them know the" fun" you had; never imagining the cost to yourself, that other person, or to God. How many times has your mouth taken you to a place which you knew better about going? Gossip? The little white lie? That sarcastic remark or negative comment? What about those times that you wanted to do wrong? (v. 1-6) Although this psalm is about a man who had done evil deeds and bragged about it, it is also a psalm about each of us. David rebukes the man for his deeds by letting him know that God was and will forever be in control.

27

No matter the misdeeds done, from the mundane to the grievous, God will judge each of us and for some, an example to be made (v. 7).

Yet as always with God, no matter the promise of retribution, He always gives us the promise of redemption. The symbolism of the olive branch (v. 8) in this scripture refers to the renewal of life, peace, and a thing of beauty. It also refers to being children of God. For those that love the Lord, the recognition of God's eternal love is something that cannot be denied (v. 8). As we reside in His house, we can take comfort that God has not forgotten His promise to each of us that follow Him and submit our lives to Him.

**Reflection & Study Questions**

**So, although God is in control, it is not a control based on fear. Instead, it is rooted in the knowledge of God's perfect love, His perfect mercy, and His perfect forgiveness. That is the true definition of trusting God.**

**1. Do you trust God? Really trust Him?**

**2. How can you show Him that you do?**

## Deliver Me

*"O LORD, do not rebuke me in Your anger, Nor chasten me in Your hot displeasure. Have mercy on me, O LORD, for I am weak; O LORD, heal me, for my bones are troubled. My soul also is greatly troubled; But You, O LORD—how long? Return, O LORD, deliver me! Oh, save me for Your mercies' sake! For in death there is no remembrance of You; In the grave who will give You thanks? I am weary with my groaning; All night I make my bed swim; I drench my couch with my tears. My eye wastes away because of grief; It grows old because of all my enemies. Depart from me, all you workers of iniquity; For the LORD has heard the voice of my weeping. The LORD has heard my supplication; The LORD will receive my prayer. Let all my enemies be ashamed and greatly troubled; Let them turn back and be ashamed suddenly." Psalm 6 NKJV*

In Psalm 6, we encounter David at a low point. He is hurt, worn out, crying to the Lord for deliverance. It has gotten so bad, that in verse 3, David asks "Lord, how long". Essentially he is asking God, "Where are you in my time of need?" He is tired of crying to the Lord. He is tired of seeing no change in his situation. It would seem as if he is tired of praying to God, because at his lowest point, David is asking God for mercy, i.e. relief. We don't know what prompted David to write this psalm or what he was encountering. He possibly could have written it at the death of his first son with Bathsheba or when his son Absalom betrayed him or any number of trials that he encountered. We don't know. But at some point, David was so broken that he questioned when God would deliver Him. And this question posed in verse 3, showed the foundation of David's faith, not the lack of it.

It is this foundation that makes Psalm 6 so important. It not only demonstrates the anguish, fear, and doubt you experience during a storm, it demonstrates the faith needed to get through the storm. In verse 5, David asks the Lord, "how can I praise you if I am gone?" In verse 4, he tells the Lord to save him. David is not only speaking as someone who has seen the merciful hand of God, David is speaking as someone standing in expectation of God moving in his life. And God did. God heard David's prayers. God listened all those nights where David felt alone with his tears. God was there in the midst of it all, even when David felt his groaning went unheeded. The foundation of David's faith was simple. He believed. He believed God would always deliver Him. Every night that he cried, He cried to the One who could deliver him. And when he didn't see deliverance coming, he still went before God and asked how much longer. He didn't try to figure it out. He didn't turn away. He just waited and prayed to God. The greatest thing David will ever be remembered for is his faith and belief in God. He believed he would be king. He believed he would kill Goliath. He believed. And that is what God is asking each of us to do.

### Reflection & Study Questions

If you are encountering, have encountered, or for when you encounter the next storm in your life, remember who and what is the foundation of your faith. The simplest thing God has asked you to do is also the hardest thing God has called you to do. Believe in who He is and what He can do.

1. What has been the hardest thing for you to believe?

2. Define "faith" and what it means to you?

3. What are ways God has called you to exhibit faith?

# Bipolar Christian

*"Beware, brethren, lest there be in any of you an evil heart of unbelief in departing from the living God; but exhort one another daily, while it is called "Today," lest any of you be hardened through the deceitfulness of sin. For we have become partakers of Christ if we hold the beginning of our confidence steadfast to the end, while it is said: "Today, if you will hear His voice, do not harden your hearts as in the rebellion." Hebrews 3:12-15 NKJV*

*"But let him ask in faith, with no doubting, for he who doubts is like a wave of the sea driven and tossed by the wind. For let not that man supposes that he will receive anything from the Lord; he is a double-minded man, unstable in all his ways." James 1:6-8 ESV*

"Bipolar Christian". This is the term one of my best friends and prayer partners called me on Friday. She said it with the best intentions and the tinkling of laughter, but it still stung. Don't get me wrong, it was funny, but it also so easily summed up who I am and what I had become, in two words.

Here recently, I acted and behaved in a manner unbecoming to God. I let my frustrations and my belief that God was not moving quickly enough in my life, to not cloud my thinking, but to push me into a path not pleasing to Him. I did it with eyes wide open. No excuses. Me being me, I manipulated and controlled the situation in order for me to receive my desired outcome (that sentence alone is a testament to my warped mind). And as I thought back to what scripture I could use to explain my actions, I came across Hebrews 3:15. Jesus plainly says to not harden your hearts in rebellion when you hear God. I did just that to prove that I could. To prove the type of woman I could become, to show the type of woman I had become. What's so sad is that my heart was hardened so much, that I felt no guilt. I feel no guilt, even now, absolutely none. But I know my actions were not pleasing to God. But, they were pleasing to me. Isn't that enough?

And yet, if I trace the hardening of my heart to that moment, I realize that I would be lying to myself. It came well before then. My rebellious spirit has been growing for not just months, but years. God has this unbelievable way of having things occur in your life, that break you so much that you have no other choice but to come to Him. God gives each of us a "wake up" call, where you have a choice to choose Him or to choose you. He nudges you with circumstances, people, His word, etc. In my crises (plural), I chose Him.

## Shaniqua Rischer

I have been so broken by God before, that it not only strengthened my faith, but led me to a greater understanding and love of Christ. But, that still didn't stop my rebellion. Instead, it grew moment by moment, disappointment by disappointment not only in me, but in God.

This time, God didn't use any catastrophic events to bring me to Him. He simply...slowly...started to remove His hand and let me have my own way. What's so funny is that I felt it and a part of me was glad that He did. I could be free to do what I wanted, speak as I wanted, and behave as I wanted without conviction, or at least, not enough conviction to remove me from my plotted course. The last time I wrote a devotional was September 25th. The time before that was June 23rd. I went from a woman seeing God in everything, being able to create full sermons in my head based on one thing to nothing. And that was not made obvious to me until last night. "I am second". For those that live in Dallas, you have seen the billboards everywhere, with the black and white picture of a person prominently displayed below the script, "I am second". For the longest, I kept seeing the billboards and telling myself I need to look it up online. I thought it was a drug rehab place or talking about people who had a second chance on life. It's not. The billboards are about you. They are about me. They are about God. I am second, because He is first. But instead of being excited about the campaign, I got angry. I was angry because I had a similar idea, a very similar and documented idea. I even submitted the outline to an organization last year, hoping to be chosen for a grant to institute it. I even purchased a domain name 2 years ago to promote it. Mine was to be called "Great is" and another one even incorporated the "I am" in the domain name. Two years ago. I was so angry, I was like who are these people. Did I make a mistake submitting my proposal to someone and did they steal my idea? Then God spoke. "No". And it became glaringly obvious, that God will get His glory in spite of me. I swallowed a bitter pill yesterday. Two years He has been speaking to me and I have ignored Him. Did I foolishly think that God only spoke to me? No, not that, but I did think I had time. That God knew I would eventually come back to Him to serve and I would do what He was calling me to do. I believed that God knowing that (because He is Omniscient) would understand. I was wrong. God did know that I would return, but that didn't mean that He would "wait" on me. How funny is that? God waiting on me. God's will, WILL be done, in spite of you too. Few feelings are as sobering as when you realize how you have let God down and in spite of you, He still, will go forward with His plans.

So, I must now contend with who I am (as I often have shown and openly shared this struggle these past few years). And that person is the "Bipolar Christian". But God, even then has already addressed and spoken on this. James 1:8 speaks on the double-minded person. I must choose again; and, I am more fully comprehending, I must choose daily. Once your heart has become hardened, it's hard to go back. You can lose innocence. You can AND will begin to view the worldly way of living as the right way. Although it is hard to erase disobedience and the consequences of sin, it is just as hard to choose to live holy. But, repeatedly throughout the Bible, God has called us to be Holy, because He is Holy. I just finished reading Leviticus (the least read book in the Bible—understandably so) and all throughout the laws and rules He gave, God repeatedly gave instructions to the Hebrews on how they should worship and sacrifice because He is Holy. Not only was I convicted, I was also overwhelmed by the sheer magnitude and detail of God's instructions. I wouldn't have made it past five years old if I lived under the old covenant. But now that I live under the New Covenant in Christ, I am not any better. My salvation is assured, but at what cost? Is the cost me living and becoming a "Bipolar Christian"??? Not only is my mind wavering, but my actions and behavior as well. I would like to say that I am tired enough of being a bipolar Christian, that I will change my spots overnight. But it won't be that easy. I must choose to daily to trust and honor God. I must choose daily to turn my thoughts, my ways, and my very act of living over to Him. I invite you to join with me as I do this. I cannot do it alone, neither do I want to.

The reason why so many Christians share their faith and speak about God is because we have learned what it means to live apart from Him and what it means to be the child of the King, brethren in Christ. It is a difficult and continuous journey. Just as I have stood in the gap for others, I need someone to stand in the gap with me and for me. I honestly want the life God wants for me; to become the woman in faith, in ministry, that He showed me.

Shaniqua Rischer

**Reflection & Study Questions**

I must ask each of you that read this, what do you want? Now, what are you willing to lose, give up, or do to get it AND to live it? I am not alone is claiming the title of a "Bipolar Christian", but I do embrace it. I embrace it because unless I see what I have become, I won't see where I am headed.

1. Do you believe you are a Bipolar Christian?

2. How have you lived a fake life as a Christian?

3. What does God desire of you to live an authentic life?

# Hidden Sin

*"Surely God is good to Israel, to those who are pure in heart. But as for me, my feet had almost slipped; I had nearly lost my foothold. For I envied the arrogant when I saw the prosperity of the wicked. They have no struggles; their bodies are healthy and strong. They are free from the burdens common to man; they are not plagued by human ills. This is what the wicked are like— always carefree, they increase in wealth. Surely in vain have I kept my heart pure; in vain have I washed my hands in innocence. All day long I have been plagued; I have been punished every morning. If I had said, "I will speak thus," I would have betrayed your children. When I tried to understand all this, it was oppressive to me till I entered the sanctuary of God; then I understood their final destiny. Yet I am always with you; you hold me by my right hand. You guide me with your counsel, and afterward you will take me into glory. Whom have I in Heaven but you? And earth has nothing I desire besides you. My flesh and my heart may fail, but God is the strength of my heart and my portion forever. Those who are far from you will perish; you destroy all who are unfaithful to you. 28 But as for me, it is good to be near God. I have made the Sovereign LORD my refuge; I will tell of all your deeds." Psalm 73:1-5, 12-17, 23-28 NIV*

There are two things that separate me from most people that I know. The first is I believe God has a calling on my life to teach and preach the Gospel (I know, can you believe it?). The second is that I am a 30-year old virgin (I know, can you believe it?). The first of which is a calling I have reluctantly accepted and the last is a fact, I have openly disregarded in shame. Despite how much I would love to deny a correlation between the two, I have to admit that God may actually have a plan. Yet, it wasn't until this week that I realized how one may in fact be hindering the other.

It was not the first time she asked me this [she being my Bible study leader] but it was perhaps the first time I took a moment to listen to the answer. The question being, what unconfessed or hidden sin do I have that is keeping me from fully walking in the purpose God has ordained for my life? Long question, short answer. My initial answer was nothing. All of my sins, I confess... ; - ) But the more I thought on it, the more it bothered me. I asked one of my prayer partners what she thought. Her answer was "you may not be fully ready and you may be in the world more than you think". That answer I could accept. It was easier to swallow because I can see the things in my life I don't want to leave behind. I tell God often, "I am trying, right?"

Again, I could accept that easy answer. It had more to do with the timing of my growing up than anything I had or had not done. But God. The next day, I was talking to a friend and what she said made me realize how far from the will of God I was. As two women sharing over dinner we could only be talking about one thing. You got it. Men. She wanted to pray for me a mate, which normally would have been fine. I'll accept prayer for that (being single, most people want to pray for you to get a man/woman anyway –they like to have you think the grass is greener). But this prayer wasn't that simple because she added one thing. She wanted to pray for a mate to enter my life and cherish me so much, he would abstain from sex until marriage for me. I looked at her crazy. Big eyes and all! How could she? How are you going to pray for what I don't want? So, I did what any sane Christian would do. I turned down her prayer and told her "No". I sure did! That simple gesture spoke more about my walk than I cared to admit. I am a person struggling to minister to others in the way God has shown me I one day will, but hasn't. I am a person that has been given a burden to speak of God, when in my heart in this area, I can't speak for God.

In the midst of these revelations, I happened to read Psalm 73 again. Verse 1 and 2 states that:

*"surely God is good…to those pure of heart, but as for me…"* It's that "but" that got me. For so long I have "envied and seen the prosperity" (verse 3) of those who are sexually active and experience a physical pleasure I crave. My hidden sin just so happens to be most others, blatant sin. While some repent and cry to God for deliverance of sexual sin, I carry an embittered heart and ask "why not me?" Those who have stepped outside the will of God with regards to sex are like those in verse 4 "strong and healthy". From the outside looking in, they have gotten away with their sins of "sexing on Saturday and praising on Sunday". I know a lot who that amply describes. I too learn by watching the walks of others. Long ago, I gave up any pride I would have in sexual purity and knew that all it would take is the right time for me (notice I didn't say person) and "all bets were off". So I hid that bitterness in my heart, not against others or even God, but against myself for as verse 14 states, "surely in vain have I kept my heart pure; in vain have I washed my hands in innocence".

So, imagine me with a vision from the Lord, ready to do His will. Sacrificially if need be (all or nothing-or so I thought), getting up daily, fearing my anointing was gone. No words have come. No doors open for working in ministry. No chapters written. I once again was asked what sin is in my life that I had not confessed. So, again, I asked God and He showed me a prayer I turned my back on. So I am led to ask you that same question. What hidden sin is blocking you from living out your anointing? What is blocking you from being a preacher, being a mentor, of living a joyful life, a blessed life-not by the standards of man, but by the blood of the Lamb? It can be pride, anger, idolatry, believing in self and not Christ, a generational curse or any number of things. Anything hidden will keep you apart from God and you may not know it. I have lived with this sin for so long, I never realized how it was eating away at my future. I always assumed when I did finally preach or write about God, that I would do it effectively balancing my "sainthood" with my "sexing" as so many fail at doing. In my ignorance (v. 22), I maligned the Father's vision for my life. It's hard to go forward when you know that yesterday, if it came down to you preaching the word of God and having your physical desires met, that God assuredly would have come in a distant second. But He holds each of us, myself included, by "our right hand and guides us with His counsel" (v. 23-24).

*Prayer: Lord, I confess my hidden sin(s) to you. For every child of God that reads this, convict them of their hidden and blatant sins, Father. Convict us of anything that separates us from you. Come into our lives Lord and show us how to walk in your light. Father, please remove the sense of complacency for sin in our lives. Please remove the sense of, I am "trying" from our lives. Deliver unto each of us the courage and the faith to know that we have been delivered and to live by that deliverance. It is only by your name, Christ Jesus, that we are more than conquerors. Amen.*

## Reflection & Study Questions

**1. What hidden sin is blocking you from living out your anointing?**

Shaniqua Rischer

## The Consequences of Sin

*"In the first month the whole Israelite community arrived at the Desert of Zin, and they stayed at Kadesh. There Miriam died and was buried. Now there was no water for the community, and the people gathered in opposition to Moses and Aaron. They quarreled with Moses and said, "If only we had died when our brothers fell dead before the LORD! Why did you bring the LORD's community into this desert, that we and our livestock should die here? Why did you bring us up out of Egypt to this terrible place? It has no grain or figs, grapevines or pomegranates. And there is no water to drink!" Moses and Aaron went from the assembly to the entrance to the Tent of Meeting and fell facedown, and the glory of the LORD appeared to them. The LORD said to Moses, "Take the staff, and you and your brother Aaron gather the assembly together. Speak to that rock before their eyes and it will pour out its water. You will bring water out of the rock for the community so they and their livestock can drink." So Moses took the staff from the LORD's presence, just as he commanded him. He and Aaron gathered the assembly together in front of the rock and Moses said to them, "Listen, you rebels, must we bring you water out of this rock?" Then Moses raised his arm and struck the rock twice with his staff. Water gushed out, and the community and their livestock drank. But the LORD said to Moses and Aaron, "Because you did not trust in me enough to honor me as holy in the sight of the Israelites, you will not bring this community into the land I give them." These were the waters of Meribah, where the Israelites quarreled with the LORD and where he showed himself holy among them." Numbers 20:1-13 NIV*

This year, in my Bible study, we have done a yearlong study of Moses. We are in the book of Numbers now. From the beginning, God has spoken to me through this study. If I wasn't relating to the Israelites in their rebellion, I was relating to Moses and his awkward acceptance of his calling. However, week by week, studying also allowed me to learn more about God. Not only did I learn about the God who is full of grace ,the God that demands respect, praise, and honor, but the God of glory as well. During the Bible study, I also learned of the terrifying wrath of God and His righteousness. I read how holy God is and how He hates sin; yet most importantly, I witnessed how God is not playing…with any of us. With all of that knowledge, you would have thought that I would have learned my lesson the first time.

*I felt no guilt the first time...*

I have wanted to go to Africa for many years (at least the past 5 years). Originally, I had planned to go for my 30th birthday and even asked someone if they would go with me about 2 years prior, so we could set up a payment plan for it. But, that didn't happen. However, I never forgot that dream. Two years ago, I decided that I would go to Africa regardless of who accompanied me and learned of a ministry program that would take people to South Africa to minister to others. In 2007, I had just left my job and in 2008, I was a new home owner, but I vowed in 2009, I would apply for the program and hopefully be accepted. My biggest fear was how I would afford the $4200 price tag. But, they always say act in preparation of your blessing, so I prepared to go. I started banking my vacation time so that I could take 2 weeks off from work this summer, I began looking for a part time job to cover the cost, and I spoke with some people about possible support financially. I acted in preparation and faith...in this. So, I finally applied and submitted my application on March 16. The application was detailed, including a resume, three references, release forms and a moral conviction questionnaire. With the exception of the questionnaire, I was confidant I would be accepted. See, in the questionnaire, they asked about your past and recent sexual history. Knowing what I had just taken part in the previous month, I was hoping they would overlook my recent infraction and look at my past abstinence history. I mean, really. A 31-yr. old virgin is something to take note of, right? LOL!

*I felt no guilt the second time...*

After submitting the application, I was convicted of the recent things I had done and knew they were not pleasing to God. Not just sexual encounters, but the rebellious nature of my heart. I understood that the devil had sown seeds of frustration and division and I gladly watered those seeds myself. My actions had nothing to do with temptation, but everything to do with the lack of patience and trusting God (I mean, exactly how LONG is "to wait"). So in spite of the word and heeding of God (speaking not only through His word but through a few of my sister friends), I still went and stepped outside the boundaries of God. Blatantly disobeying Him and throwing it in His face.

*I felt no guilt the third time, but God…*

Not too long after the 2nd time of rebellion, I set-up the 3rd encounter. 1:30 am. Can you say it was about to be on and poppin? I remember saying, God just don't let me catch anything. See, I had it all planned and was in control (as usual). I knew what time he was getting here and this time, I wasn't going to tell him he had to leave before morning either. It was Spring Break. I would get to work whenever I wanted the next day. But, God had other plans for me. So much so, that my plans were delayed/canceled/and put on the back burner. I was not thrilled (especially with how the door was closed), because I thought it was about to be…on and poppin!!!

*Sin…*

The same day I set-up my rendezvous, I spoke with the leader of the mission trip I had applied for (and also had prayed for forgiveness of my previous weekend escapade-to quote my home girl, "cuz, I am a sinner"). All of my paperwork had been received, everything was in order, and I would have my letter on Friday via e-mail. I was excited because without saying I was accepted, I was accepted. So on Friday, when I received a call concerning my moral conviction questionnaire from a female organization member, I knew it was a formality. Or so I thought. As the conversation went on, doubt crept in. She was asking detailed questions, but nothing I couldn't handle. I had explained everything that happened a few months ago and how I got to that point, but my spirit whispered…what about a few days ago??? The longer we stayed on the phone, the more doubt I had. But, I gave it to God, because I knew what would be, would be. And then, it was revealed. My past indiscretions weren't as much in my past as the application would have led her to believe.

*The Consequence of Sin…*

After I got off the call, I received another phone call about 45-minutes later from the mission leader. He wanted to talk to me, but I wasn't in a place to talk in-depth so he asked to call me later. I agreed and was feeling great. I knew I had cinched it. I had got in. So, when I spoke with him at 5:30 on Friday, I wasn't surprised when he said "based on your resume, you are perfect. Your application is exactly what I am looking for and I even had submitted your name to the system to purchase your flight earlier." I was surprised when he continued by saying, "However, I can't offer you admittance to the program. According to the recommendation of 'X' with your moral interview, she feels now wouldn't be the time for you to attend." Words can't begin to sum up what I felt. And in that moment I knew what my consequence was. I wasn't going on a trip I had prayed for years to attend (because of the last 3 months). I wasn't about to be anybody's witness. It wasn't just my recent interludes I had experienced that disqualified me. It was the disobedience. It was the rebellion. It was the lack of trust. It was the lack of patience. You see, God called my bluff. And He called it in such a way that there was NO DOUBT as to why I wasn't admitted. One single act…

*Moses & Numbers 20…*

After Moses experience with "I AM" (God) at the burning bush, the Bible records the actions of Moses and the Israelites for the next 42-years. The Israelites were the most rebellious people you can imagine. God gave them chance, after chance, after chance. And when that failed, God got "OG". He threatened many times to wipe them off the face of the earth. Indeed, some He consumed in fire, some He opened the earth to swallow whole, and some were killed by the plague. Through this all, Moses remained His faithful and obedient servant. Moses never missed a beat. Never, that is, until Numbers 20. In Numbers 20, Moses did what most of us, myself included, would call a simple oversight. He followed God's directions, but only partially. However, as was reiterated tonight, even partial obedience, is still disobedience. That disobedience caused Moses not to enter the Promise Land. One thing. One simple thing.

*My conviction…*

Even after Friday, no matter how hurt I was, I told myself I was taking this like a big girl and wouldn't cry over spilled milk. Remember I told God before my sin that whatever consequence I was to have, I would handle it (just please don't let me catch anything). I told God that… Since Friday, I have been acting as if everything is ok. And for the most part it was, but I wasn't going to get off that easy. See, I still didn't truly repent. God had yet

41

to finish speaking to my heart and my spirit. I had yet to read and understand Numbers 20. I had yet to go to Bible study and hear tonight's lecture. I had yet to hear someone say that those who are leaders ARE held under different accountability. I had yet to understand that if you don't have a consequence, you will do it again, until you become proficient in that sin-until you have a true reckoning. I had yet to hear that every person and every life is important to God, but that sin will limit your usefulness to God. I had yet to hear...

*My devotional...*

I had yet to hear it, but hopefully not you. I didn't write all of these words or my business to just share. A long time ago, when I first heard God's calling on my life, someone asked was I supposed to be a preacher. I said no, because I knew God called me to be something much worse in my eyes. I was to be a prophet. Not a person to predict what is to come, but a person who is to proclaim the word of God to those who didn't want to hear it. I am a sinner, but now, I want to for once say what God has told me to say out of reverence to Him (ain't no telling what tomorrow will bring). Years ago I told my friends I was afraid of what people would say or think if I said half the stuff God told me to say, but not today...

God does not excuse sin. There is a consequence for every sin. If I thought my denial to the program was just because of physical intimacies, I could swallow that one a little better. But again, it was about all of the sin (before and after) that manifested itself in that manner.

Even though Moses didn't get to see the Promised Land, God didn't love him any less. He doesn't love me any less. He doesn't love you any less. In fact, even with all of that, He loved us so much he gave us Jesus. "For God so loved the world that He gave His only begotten Son, that whoever believes in Him shall not perish, but have eternal life. (John 3:16)

Pray for me, Me....the sinner, the bipolar Christian, the beloved daughter of the Most High God...

**Reflection & Study Questions**

**1. Are you struggling with sexual sin?**

2. What are some of the consequences that you have experienced from sin?

3. Do you feel the consequences (punishment) for your sin has matched the sin (crime)? Why or why not?

4. What did you learn from consequences you have experienced? Did you change and do better (repent)?

# Chapter 3: Adolescence – Let It Go

## Let It Go!

*"A servant cannot be corrected by mere words; though he understands, he will not respond."* *Proverbs 29:19 NKJV*

On the day I was writing this devotional, I wondered what I would say. Not because the Word doesn't have something for me to say, but because my heart is not right. Since last week, there has been a discontent in my heart that I am harboring and in some ways it gets better and in some ways it has gotten worse. The daily devotional series that my former professor writes has been focusing on forgiveness and I have struggled with reading it every day that week. I can't wait to read tomorrows because the topic is what I am struggling with forgiving someone who doesn't even think they need forgiveness. But that is tomorrow and right now I am living in today. The verse that keeps replaying in my mind is Proverbs 29: 19, "a servant cannot be corrected by mere words; though he understands, he will not respond." That gave me pause because that simple sentence, said so much. The wisdom of the Word of God.

I cannot change people. I cannot make someone give freely of themselves, just because I do it with them. They may understand, but that doesn't mean they will respond. Just because I tell someone what friendship and family means to me, doesn't mean they will automatically cherish what I cherish. Although I don't think there is anything wrong with me expecting that, there is something wrong if both parties don't view the bond that built those expectations the same way. So, I learned, mere words will not make someone respond.

You cannot change people. How many of us have watched a friend or family member walk a path that leads to destruction? A path that is obvious to everybody and sometimes, even them. We can plead, we can yell, we can cry, we can say all sort of things, but WE cannot change that person. They don't respond and it hurts us, because it is not just about them. We have vested something in them as well. There is a saying that "no man is an island" and if that is true everything someone does or does not will have ripple effects. I think we have all lived enough of life to know the truth of that statement.

But, the Word of GOD said mere words cannot correct anyone. If God said that, it made me think, what can? God has said in Proverbs 18:21 that life and death are in the power of the tongue. Since God never contradicts Himself, I had to wonder and I need to know; what does it take for someone to respond? And then it hit me. It takes me letting go. Letting go, so that God can step in and do what He deems necessary. I can't stop it, I can't delay it, and I can't make the outcome be what I want it to be. Only God can do what He will do. Although this devotional is personal to me, I am not the only one who needs to let something go. It can be a job, a relationship, a friendship, a lifestyle, or an ideal…something.

Letting go is so hard because it leaves us alone. That person, that thing, filled a space that God wants to fill. And that person, who is in need of correction, they won't get it if you are always there to point it out, to pick them up, or to give them mere words. It takes something higher than you. It takes God.

**Reflection & Study Questions**

**1. Who or what do you need to let go?**

**2. Why are you still holding on to them?**

Shaniqua Rischer

## Hidden Shame

*"We are pushed hard from all sides. But we are not beaten down. We are bewildered. But that doesn't make us lose hope. Others make us suffer. But God does not desert us. We are knocked down. But we are not knocked out. We always carry around the death of Jesus in our bodies. In that way, the life of Jesus can be shown in our bodies. We who are alive are always in danger of death because we are serving Jesus. So his life can be shown in our earthly bodies. Death is at work in us. But life is at work in You. It is written, "I believed, and so I have spoken." (Psalm 116:10) "With that same spirit of faith we also believe. And we also speak. We know that God raised the Lord Jesus from the dead. And he will also raise us up with Jesus. He will bring us with you to God in Heaven. All of that is for your benefit. God's grace is reaching more and more people. So they will become more and more thankful. They will give glory to God. We don't give up. Our bodies are becoming weaker and weaker. But our spirits are being renewed day by day. Our troubles are small. They last only for a short time. But they are earning for us a glory that will last forever. It is greater than all our troubles. So we don't spend all our time looking at what we can see. Instead, we look at what we can't see. What can be seen lasts only a short time. But what can't be seen will last forever." 2 Corinthians 4:8-18 NIRV*

Yesterday, a friend of mine had the courage to ask for prayer for something they had been struggling with for 12 years (sounds like the unnamed woman in the in the Bible, now that I think about it). They are at their wits end in carrying this burden, but as we know, sometimes it's when we finally speak on it and no longer allow it to be hidden in the shadows, that it no longer has control over us. It is then that we can really submit something to God and trust ourselves enough to leave it there. I pray that they finally either receive deliverance or the peace of God (Jehovah Shalom) with the outcome. Being the season of change we are in, I believe change is coming their way. Now, they just have to have faith to live the life God calls for them.

I have another friend who seems to be bound by decisions and choices in life that may sometimes seem as chains, but what they fail to realize it is not the decisions and choices that chain them. It is they. Although you can have joy without happiness, it is better to have both. They said the journey of a thousand miles starts with the first step. Well, living according to God's purpose starts with faith. However, they too are in the midst of a change, because they cannot hide from God any longer. I pray that my friend has the faith to do the unthinkable, which is surrender to God and follow wherever

He leads. I have never seen Him contradict himself and His word has always been the compass for each of us to follow.

Although I have never had sexual intercourse, I am a victim of sexual abuse. My experiences are so "flimsy"; I often wonder can it be considered abuse and not just youthful playing with a friend or a stranger. But then, I remember the shame, fear, and silence I have housed in me for longer than I care to remember and ask myself, "Can I term it anything else?" Fast forward years and I remember the taunts boys, trying to be men, said to me on school house steps. How one in particular used to corner me…to touch me, without my consent. How he made me feel dirty and ashamed to be the woman I was becoming. Even as an adult, I tried to understand why some men approached me in a sexually disrespectful manner. Like they knew something about me, I didn't. Those experiences shaped and changed my psyche. I know why I have sought intimacy with "unavailable" men. I know why I used to shy away from touching and being touched. I understand why I was the woman I was yesterday. But I also understand who I am today. Even when I didn't know it, He was watching over me, even when I didn't "feel" it, He held me.

But what ties our three stories together? Brokenness? Choices? Redemption? Faith? Those four powerful words all lay at the feet of Jesus . We may be hard pressed, but not crushed. We may be perplexed, but not in despair (v. 8-10, NIV). We may be broken, but we are not beyond healing. We may suffer, but the suffering is never in vain. God, Jesus, and the Cross can change your life (v. 10-12). I do not speak from someone else's testimony, I speak from my own. I said it before and I will say it again, you do not have to accept the ugly. Therefore, what do you need to lay at His feet today? My wish and prayer for each of you is to deepen your relationship with God. Read the Bible. Pray. Get on your knees. Know who Christ is to you, for the world will have you think He was just a man, but He wasn't. He was God in the flesh and He is arisen. The world is not going to get any easier or better. Look around and know that truth. As a matter of fact, a lot of Christ followers are being attacked this year. God is building and strengthening His army for a reason. The battle is a spiritual one. And the only way to have life is through Christ. If you don't know Him, seek Him. He will always meet you.

**Reflection & Study Questions**

**1. What do you need to lay at His feet today? Be open and honest with Him if with no one else. He will listen to you.**

# In The Shelter of the Most High

*"He who dwells in the shelter of the Most High will rest in the shadow of the Almighty. I will say of the LORD, "He is my refuge and my fortress, my God, in whom I trust." Surely he will save you from the fowler's snare and from the deadly pestilence. He will cover you with his feathers, and under his wings you will find refuge; his faithfulness will be your shield and rampart. You will not fear the terror of night, nor the arrow that flies by day, nor the pestilence that stalks in the darkness, nor the plague that destroys at midday. A thousand may fall at your side, ten thousand at your right hand, but it will not come near you. You will only observe with your eyes and see the punishment of the wicked. If you make the Most High your dwelling—even the LORD, who is my refuge-then no harm will befall you, no disaster will come near your tent. For he will command his angels concerning you to guard you in all your ways; they will lift you up in their hands, so that you will not strike your foot against a stone. You will tread upon the lion and the cobra; you will trample the great lion and the serpent. "Because he loves me," says the LORD, "I will rescue him; I will protect him, for he acknowledges my name. He will call upon me, and I will answer him; I will be with him in trouble, I will deliver him and honor him. With long life will I satisfy him and show him my salvation." Psalm 91 NIV*

When I read this psalm, so many things went through my mind, so many ways I could approach the Word of God. Usually I write psalms through my own personal testimonies and I was tempted to do that this time. I am a firm believer that only someone who knows you intimately can speak intimately about you. That is the reason I so often speak of Jesus in terms as He relates to me. Although it's hard, I am transparent because I have experienced the hand of God in my life at my darkest hours and the most joyous. So, as I read this psalm I kept coming back to verse 1, "He who dwells in the shelter of the Most High will rest in the shadow of the Almighty."

Langston Hughes wrote once, "life ain't been no crystal staircase" in a poem about a mother imparting wisdom to her son. We are at the half way point of this year and for some this year has been trying as their life has taken turns and twists that only God could foresee. For others, this year has been a much needed reprieve from the previous trials and tribulations they have experienced. One thing is clear, as each day passes; it becomes more apparent that we all could say those same words to any of our own loved ones.

Yet for those who know God intimately, they recognize that in spite of life's difficulties there comes a time when you face God and come to understand what it means to dwell in the shelter of the Most High. For those who dwell in the shelter of God, they know that there are many dark nights, but those same nights are experienced in the hand of the Lord. For those who dwell in the shelter of the Most High, they know that there will be times when they lose everything, only to find everything in Him. But how do they know? Simple; they trust Him. Totally, fearfully…trustfully.

When you trust God, "a thousand may fall at your side" (v.7), but you will still be standing. If you make the Most High your shelter, "he will command his angels concerning you to guard you in all your ways" (v. 11). The journey of a thousand miles begins with one step. The journey to trusting God begins with one tragedy. But it doesn't end there for "he who dwells in the shelter of the Most High will rest in the shadow of the Almighty."

*Prayer: Father, thank You for every tragedy and for every joy for without it, I would not have the faith that I do. Yet more importantly Father, thank You for keeping me in those midnight hours when there was no one but You and Your angels. I felt You then. I feel You know. For those who don't know You, hold them close and for those that do, may they continue to dwell in Your shelter and rest in Your glory.*

**Reflection & Study Questions**

**1. Do you caste your cares upon God?**

**2. From what do you need God to provide shelter for you?**

# Life Is About Choices

*"Elijah went before the people and said, "How long will you waver between two opinions? If the LORD is God, follow him; but if Baal is God, follow him." But the people said nothing." 1 Kings 18:21 NIV*

I have been reading about Elijah, the Old Testament prophet, and it has been very interesting. Elijah had a single minded commitment to God through various trials and tribulations. I Kings and II Kings chronicles Elijah's life. He was an instrument of God during some very difficult times/situations. God sent him as a prophet during the times of King Ahab and his wife Jezebel. He would pronounce a drought on the land that would last three years; he spoke against Jezebel acting in the Kings name and killing Naboth for his land; and he spoke against the worship of idols and gods. But that's not what makes this story so personal to me at this time; what makes it personal is that he made a conscious decision to follow God and Jezebel/Ahab made a conscious decision to act against God and His prophet.

*Life is all about choices.*

Today, my mood is not the best, not the best by a LONG shot. It's only 10 days into the new year and I have had to deal with issues that will affect me seriously financially (and it's not even about my addiction to shopping that's caused this or me mismanaging money), I have had to deal with disappointment, I have had to deal with the fact that I am currently waiting on my grandfather to die. Today, I have had to deal with 4 separate incidents today at work. ALL of which has made me want to go off on someone and mind you I got to work at 10 am (late) and it's now only 1:30. And I know I am not the only person. I can count at least 2 of you on here that has had to deal with SERIOUS illness in your parents, 1 who has had a sick grandmother, not to mention all of the other hurts, disappointments, etc. that we all have dealt with.

*But, life is about choices.*

Elijah chose to follow God, despite persecution from the King, despite feeling alone, depressed, etc. Let's not forget how Jezebel and King Ahab chose to defy God, despite how many times God warned them, gave them second and third chances. More importantly, they chose to defy God's prophet IN SPITE of the demonstration of God's power. I mean, God caused a drought for three years, caused a fire to consume Elijah's burnt offering before their eyes, and then made it rain. He even spoke the death of over 100 men and slain over 450 false prophets. I mean, I have gotten some clues before that I have ignored… But…

*Life is about choices.*

My point, each day, I choose what I will do. Each day, I choose how I will react to whatever new is brought my way. I was asked in December by a good friend about my faith and how/why I view life as I do. My faith and my walk are built around a choice. The other night, someone told me that my good mood was depressing sometimes. I told him I struggle and have hurts, disappointments just like him. That I have bad days and am depressed and feel like life has kicked me at my lowest; that even though I have those moments and have lived through those days, that for some reason, I can never stay that way for long. He said "good for you". I take it not everyone is like that. But, everyone has a choice. So, today and for this year and in all that you do, remember it's a choice. Every thought, every action, every reaction is a choice. I hope you choose wisely.

**Reflection & Study Questions**

**1. Do you struggle with depression? Clinical depression is a chemical imbalance that should be addressed and discussed with a physician and/or licensed counselor. However, some depression is the result of negative thoughts that we have allowed to take root and influence our actions.**

**2. How can you make better choices in life and respond to better to situations as they arise?**

# Judas: Betrayer and Beloved

*"Then one of the Twelve—the one called Judas Iscariot—went to the chief priests and asked, "What are you willing to give me if I hand him over to you?" So they counted out for him thirty silver coins. From then on Judas watched for an opportunity to hand him over..." Matthew 26:14-16 NIV*

*"When evening came, Jesus was reclining at the table with the Twelve. And while they were eating, he said, "I tell you the truth, one of you will betray me." They were very sad and began to say to him one after the other, "Surely not I, Lord?" Jesus replied, "The one who has dipped his hand into the bowl with me will betray me. The Son of Man will go just as it is written about him. But woe to that man who betrays the Son of Man! It would be better for him if he had not been born." Then Judas, the one who would betray him, said, "Surely not I, Rabbi?" Jesus answered, "Yes, it is you."..." Matthew 26:20-25 NIV*

*"While he was still speaking, Judas, one of the Twelve, arrived. With him was a large crowd armed with swords and clubs, sent from the chief priests and the elders of the people. Now the betrayer had arranged a signal with them: "The one I kiss is the man; arrest him." Going at once to Jesus, Judas said, "Greetings, Rabbi!" and kissed him. Jesus replied, "Friend, do what you came for." Matthew 26:47-50 NIV*

*"When Judas, who had betrayed him, saw that Jesus was condemned; he was seized with remorse and returned the thirty silver coins to the chief priests and the elders. I have sinned," he said, "for I have betrayed innocent blood." "What is that to us?" they replied. "That's your responsibility." So Judas threw the money into the temple and left. Then he went away and hanged himself." Matthew 27:3-5 NIV*

A few weeks ago, my friends and I had an interesting conversation about what it means to be saved. Some stated that you can "prove" you are saved through your deeds/work for the kingdom and others responded that only Christ can judge your heart, but the only way to be saved is to confess your belief in Jesus Christ as the Son of God who died on the cross for your sins and was resurrected. It led to a lively debate about basic Christian doctrine. I believe the latter, not the former. My salvation is based on my belief and not anything I can "do" for Jesus or myself for that matter. But it made me pause, why would someone think that our deeds can influence our salvation? It was then, that I thought back to Judas, the one known as the Betrayer of Christ and who I believe was one of the most loved of Christ.

*Being in His presence, but...*

Judas is the perfect example of one who walked so closely with Christ, but still knew Him not. He saw Jesus feed the 5,000; he was there when Christ walked on water; when He raised Lazarus; and healed the sick not only by laying hands, but simply speaking healing into existence. Judas was there during all of that and by sight, some would say he was "saved". He walked with Christ, talked with Christ, and even served with Christ, but he did not know Him personally and fully. In Mark 9:14-29, we see Jesus perform a great healing of the boy possessed by evil spirits. What's so interesting in this story is not that Christ performed yet another miracle. It's interesting because of what His disciples could NOT do. They didn't have the faith to heal the boy. Judas was one of those disciples. He couldn't do the very thing Jesus had instructed him to do. Why? Jesus told him and all the disciples – it took faith and prayer. Judas teaches us that you can imitate a walk with Christ and still not know Him, still not believe in Him, and still not act in faith. Do you know someone like that? Perhaps it's you?

*Betrayal...*

Everybody knows the story of Judas. He is one of the most well-known figures in the Bible for the one inexplicable and unfathomable act, the betrayal of Jesus. Matthew 26 – 27 gives a detailed account of how Judas went to the chief priest and sold Jesus to them for 30 pieces of silver. Thirty pieces. And Jesus knew it. Jesus knew intimately His chosen twelve. In John 1:35-50, John introduces each of the first disciples and how they came to know Jesus. Two followed because John the Baptist told them who Christ was, others followed because of family or friends, but Jesus knew them all. He knew their short comings, he knew their heart, he knew their temperament, and he knew what they would become. He even knew the one that would betray Him. Yet He still called Judas to serve with Him. Jesus shows us how you can love and lead, even those that will or have betrayed you. Betrayal doesn't stop your ministry to them; betrayal is why you minister more closely to them.

Christ gave us the perfect example of how we can be hurt by someone, but still forgive them. Even in Judas' betrayal, Christ had a plan. Christ's plan was not only for redemption via the Cross, but a plan that showed forgiveness as well. Even as Judas came to seal his betrayal with a kiss (Luke

22:47-48), Christ didn't treat him with condemnation, instead He instructed Judas to continue with what He came to do. When someone hurts us, they are often misled or acting out of fear and hurt. Our reaction may start in anger, but it needs to end in forgiveness. This cannot be done without Christ, the author of the blueprint for forgiveness. The betrayal of Judas allowed each person to know Christ for themselves. What Judas meant for evil, Christ (God) used for good (Genesis 50:20). Even as we are betrayed, we must lay the betrayal and the betrayer at the Cross never forgetting the end goal – forgiveness and redemption.

*Apart…*

Lastly, the greatest and saddest lesson that Judas can teach us is not one of betrayal, it's one of dying apart from Christ. After the betrayal of Christ, the Bible reports that Judas died alone and hung himself (Matthew 27:1-6), but he didn't have to die. Even if he had betrayed Christ, Judas failed to recognize the characteristics of Christ that made Him fully God; His grace and His mercy; and His abundant love and forgiveness. Jesus never turned His back on anyone that sought Him, that needed Him, no matter the crime. In our finite minds, that's hard to process. No matter the sin, Jesus forgave.

Yet Judas failed to seek Christ and ask for forgiveness. That perhaps is the greatest lesson we can learn from Judas. Not how to abstain from betrayal, because if we are honest, we have all betrayed someone that loved and cared for us. But that we cannot live our life apart from Christ. Depression. Pride. Regret. Remorse. All are chains that the devil used to keep Judas separated from Christ. They are tools He still uses today with us. Judas died not knowing the forgiveness of Christ and the chance for eternal life. You don't have to.

At the beginning, I wrote that I believed that Judas was one of Christ's most beloved disciples. Not because of what He did, but because of what He didn't do. Christ grieves every time we allow the enemy to control us and not allow ourselves to be filled with the Spirit. God grieves every time one of His children fails to come to Him – with any problem. God grieves every time He sees His children hurt or even when we pay for the consequence of our action. God, too, grieves and that grief is rooted in the deepest, purest love. Love for the lost. Love for the broken hearted. Love for those who have done wrong.  In God's eyes, we all have.  Years ago, I received a card in the mail and I saved it to remind myself of this:

*"If our greatest need had been information, GOD would have sent us an Educator,*

*If our greatest need had been technology, GOD would have sent us a Scientist,*

*If our greatest need had been money, God would have sent us an Economist,*

*If our greatest need had been for pleasure, God would have sent us an Entertainer,*

*But our GREATEST need was for forgiveness, SO GOD SENT US A SAVIOUR."*

*– Roy Lessin*

No matter the sin, no matter what you think or believe, neither Judas' betrayal nor Christ's cross were in vain.  Take part in that forgiveness.


**Reflection & Study Questions**

**1. Have you accepted forgiveness from Christ for ALL of your sins?**

**2. If not, what is holding you back?**

# God Answers Prayers

*"Hear me, O God, as I voice my complaint; protect my life from the threat of the enemy. Hide me from the conspiracy of the wicked, from that noisy crowd of evildoers. They sharpen their tongues like swords and aim their words like deadly arrows. They shoot from ambush at the innocent man; they shoot at him suddenly, without fear. They encourage each other in evil plans, they talk about hiding their snares; they say, "Who will see them?" They plot injustice and say, "We have devised a perfect plan!" Surely the mind and heart of man are cunning. But God will shoot them with arrows; suddenly they will be struck down. He will turn their own tongues against them and bring them to ruin; all who see them will shake their heads in scorn. All mankind will fear; they will proclaim the works of God and ponder what he has done. Let the righteous rejoice in the LORD and take refuge in him; let all the upright in heart praise him!" Psalm 64 NIV*

Every time I read this psalm, I think about the last 6 months of my life from a professional stand point. I took great risk, some would call foolish, by leaving my job. I even went one step further by maintaining my final commitment to a job that no longer paid me; only to be disrespected in the end by those who thought they were in a position of power. So, when I read this, I could identify with David as he speaks about his enemies, the conspiracy of the wicked, and their plots for injustice. Through my most recent testimony, I too could write those words. Yet, David didn't end his psalm there. Instead, he wrote verse 7 and this psalm became a testimony to how prayer and faith in God, can turn even the most bleak situations around. In fact, God will use the very same tools that some will use to destroy you, against them. How amazing is that? Man, may think they have the last word, but God has always been able to put a comma, where most thought to put a period. So, for those of you who understand what it means to be attacked, God can answer your prayer. You may not even feel attacked. Instead, you may feel overlooked for the job you do; again, God, can answer your prayer. Someone may be writing you out of the equation, but God can answer your prayer. Your prayer could be a prayer of deliverance, recognition, or simple strength to endure.

## Reflection & Study Questions

Shaniqua Rischer

**1. God can answer your prayer. For those who serve the Lord, the prayers of the righteous do avail much. I am a witness. Pray, and He will answer. Have you prayed to Him today?**

# Is It Fear or Faith

*The Bible says that God has not given us the spirit of fear (2 Timothy 1:7). Fear is not from God; it is the devil's tool to keep people from enjoying their lives and making progress". Fear causes a person to run, retreat, or shrink back. The Bible says in Hebrews 10:38 that we are to live by faith and not draw back in fear-and if we do draw back in fear, God's soul has no delight in us. That does not mean that God does not love us; it simply means that He is disappointed because He wants us to experience all of the good things He has in His plan for us. We can receive from God only by faith." Joyce Myers, "The Confident Woman"*

For as long as I can remember, I have been living in fear…**as long as I can remember**. To look at me, to talk to me, you wouldn't know (initially) how my spirit has been infected with this disease, but it is. Fear has wrapped it's self around my psyche and has influenced every thought and every decision I have ever made in one area of my life. It has distorted my vision, it has caused me to run (literally) and retreat, it has caused me to shoot down and shut out the possibility of God so many times. Fear has left me emotionless at times and fighting me and whoever else the other times. Fear has crippled and damaged me.

Ironically, in any other thing or area, I can and have acted/walked in absolute faith and trusted God. I have overcome and walked in faith so many times except in this area. I talk a great talk and I believe that all things are possible, but this week, this year, God has shown me a hypocrite when I looked in the mirror. He, in His love, grace, and mercy, has shown me I can no longer live a lie. I will both live (and love) in the spirit of faith or I will live (and die) in the spirit of fear. I am writing this because I don't want you to miss out on whatever God has for you because of fear. Many of us are not living up to our potential and possibilities because we are fearful, but today, I want you to know how powerful you are and how powerful I am. In addition, how powerful El Elyon says we are.

*I am a new creature in Christ:*

"The Spirit of the LORD will come powerfully upon you, and you will prophesy with them; and you will be changed into a different person."  1 Samuel 10:6 NIV

## Shaniqua Rischer

*I will fear nothing:*

"Even though I walk through the darkest valley, I will fear no evil, for you are with me; your rod and your staff, they comfort me." Psalm 23:4 NIV

*I will speak life:*

"The tongue has the power of life and death, and those who love it will eat its fruit." Proverbs 18:21 NIV

"I will boldly testify. "But you will receive power when the Holy Spirit comes on you; and you will be my witnesses in Jerusalem, and in all Judea and Samaria, and to the ends of the earth." Acts 1:8 NIV

*I have overcome AND I am a conqueror:*

"You are of God, little children, and have overcome them, because He who is in you is greater than he who is in the world." 1 John 4:4 NASB

"Yet in all these things we are more than conquerors through Him who loved us." Romans 8:37 NKJV

*I will…in His name:*

"In that day you will no longer ask me anything. Very truly I tell you, my Father will give you whatever you ask in my name. Until now you have not asked for anything in my name. Ask and you will receive, and your joy will be complete." John 16:23-24 NIV

My prayer for you this day is to be the man or woman God has called you to be. Don't live to YOUR fullest potential, LIVE TO GOD'S FULLEST POTENTIAL FOR YOU. Start that business. Be that leader. Follow that possibility.

*Prayer: I cast out this spirit of fear myself in Jesus' name. I lay hands on myself in Jesus' name. I speak life into myself in Jesus' name. Where fear has crippled and damaged, I am embracing faith to heal and restore. I trust You Lord. Amen.*

**Reflection & Study Questions**

**1. What passions do you have that have not been fulfilled due to fear and lack of faith in God?**

**2. What actions can you take to build your faith and to understand God wants the best for you?**

Shaniqua Rischer

## Broken, But Not Beyond Repair

*"So they will say, "This land that was desolate has become like the Garden of Eden; and the wasted, desolate, and ruined cities are now fortified and inhabited." Then the nations which are left all around you shall know that I, the Lord, have rebuilt the ruined places and planted what was desolate. I, the Lord, have spoken it, and I will do it." Ezekiel 36:35-36 NKJV*

"You are not good enough." "No one will ever love you." "You're ugly." "You're weak." "You should know better." "If (blank) ever found out what I did." "You...You...You." When I was a child I used to hear those words, not because of anything my parents said to me, but because of what the enemy said to me. Whenever something happened those words would be whispered into my spirit as if they were truth. As I got older, the enemy no longer needed to whisper them to me. I said them to myself. The closer I have become to God, the more insidious those words have become, sneaking up on me when I least expect. You may know what I am talking about. You may have heard the same things. The enemy seeks to kill, steal, and destroy everything about you. He can even attempt to destroy your mind and sometimes the greatest battle is not always outward, but within ourselves. The battle for your mind is the gateway to the battle for your spirit I have learned. I was once a broken person in the midst of such a battle. Broken, but not damaged. That is what God sees when He looks at each of us. He sees a broken person. A person without faith would regard "damaged" as something or someone beyond repair, but a "Person of Faith" knows that something or someone broken can be repaired, healed, and redeemed. Yet, redemption and healing don't come because you wish it so nor is it is a solitary act to be played out, instead it is a battle that can only be won by the strength of the Lord.

In the 36th Chapter of Ezekiel, God is speaking to a nation of broken people that have defamed Him and themselves. He is speaking to a nation that has been devastated, laid to waste, desolate and ravaged by others and their own personal choices. They are a nation full of people that felt as if they were cast off and unworthy of anything, let alone love, grace, mercy or redemption. God was speaking to a people very much like you and I. People that know what it feels like to think you are unworthy or to wonder how anyone, let alone God, could love you or even respect you if they knew the true you. Just as I once felt, you too may feel defeated or feel as if you are a walking wasteland. But God would have each of us to know that we are redeemed and that He has rebuilt us inside out.

In Ezekiel 36:35-36, God states in spite of everything, they are not so damaged that they cannot be restored. Yes, they have been disobedient. Yes, their cities have been devastated and their lives in ruins. Yes, other nations and the enemy has mocked them, taking pleasure in their demise. In spite of all of that, God testified that when He cleanses them, He would rebuild the cities and make the desolate land like the Garden of Eden. If God did that for the cities of Israel, what more will He do for our mind, our heart, and our spirit? Where do you need rebuilding? Where do you need cleansing?

If you are a follower of Christ, you are neither a wasteland nor a ruined vessel; you are neither less than or beyond the healing of God; instead you are more valuable than the most precious stones. So valuable, that you were bought and cleansed with the highest price, Christ's blood. God can restore even the most barren place if you allow Him.

The next time the enemy tries to gain a foothold in your thoughts or your own inner voice speaks that you are not worthy or are damaged, remember that Christ died for you, paid for you. The greatest love you will ever know is the Father's love and in that love you are redeemed and restored.

**Reflection & Study Questions**

**1. Although you have areas in your life that are damaged, can see them being repaired and restored?**

**2. Have you asked the Lord to mend the broken pieces or are trying to fix it? Why?**

Shaniqua Rischer

## The Line Has Been Drawn

*"But if serving the LORD seems undesirable to you, then choose for yourselves this day whom you will serve, whether the gods your ancestors served beyond the Euphrates, or the gods of the Amorites, in whose land you are living. But as for me and my household, we will serve the LORD." Joshua 24:15 NIV*

There comes a point in every person's life that you should grow-up (notice I didn't say will grow-up). When you grow-up, you make a conscious choice to do grown-up activities. You choose to hold down a job you may not like in order to provide for yourself and/or your family. You choose to go to sleep at a "decent" hour so that you can be fully productive the next day. You choose. Well, recently, I chose to grow-up in another way, a spiritual way. I have drawn a line, separating a before and after, in my faith walk.

In November of 2010, my accountability partner and I decided to stop asking God for money and financial blessings. We had been praying and asking for so long, from the outside you would think we did not believe He could or would give us money, even though He had met our financial needs countless times before. Well, one day we got tired of praying for the same thing, so, we stopped. We simply said, "God you know and we trust you". To some it may seem like it should be a simple prayer or a simple thing to do, but that act of maturity took years to cultivate and understand. Four-months later and we still haven't asked for anything financial and you know what? We have not needed to. God has literally blessed our finances to the point that everything is taken care of. We still have things unexpected that come up and make us wonder how it will be taken care of, but before we can even ask, it is provided. Our bills are getting paid with the same resources as before with some extra this time around.

A simple act of turning my mind away from constant asking has led to my renewed commitment to not be double-minded in my words, in my walk, and in my ministry. In Joshua 24:15, Joshua is addressing the children of Israel who were one generation removed from Egypt. Speaking to them concerning their past bondage and slavery. He is speaking to the very people that saw the parting of the Red Sea, who experienced manna from Heaven; people whose parents fought to gain their promised land of God. Although Joshua and the Israelites all experienced the same trials and tribulations, Joshua is making a stand for God, when obviously many of the Israelites are not. He drew a line of faith and stood by it. Joshua has experienced many grown-up moments before. He was called to scout out the promise land and report back to Moses what he found; he was called to lead the people of Israel after Moses died into the promise land, he was called to fight, and he was called to victory. Yet, in this one statement, Joshua made a stand that would forever separate him from his fans, his friends, and the world. Joshua stood firm and stated that he and his house would serve the Lord. He chooses to follow God through hardship, through being an outcast, through being thought crazy. If there was ever any doubt before, from that moment on, there would be none. Any double-mindedness ceased to exist.

We are all at different walks in our lives in this world and in the spiritual world. Some live and walk a life of spiritual maturity and some simply do not. One day, you will have to choose. You will have to choose Who you will follow. You will no longer be able to live the life of a double-agent. You will no longer be able to have one foot with God and the other with the author of deceit; sexual immorality; idol worship; and pride…Sin. You will have to choose what it means to follow Him wholeheartedly, in spite of hardship, loss, and even pain. You will have to choose what you believe about you and about our God. You will have to choose who you serve.

Each day, in-spite of falling down at times, I am walking by a higher level of faith. And each day, I am a little bit further than I was before. The other day, I drew a line in my faith, a before and after. Will you do the same?

## Reflection & Study Questions

**1. Do you live and walk a life of spiritual maturity and simply live life?**

**2. Do you choose live your life as you see fit or by His standards?**

**3. When will you draw the line and begin to put your life in His hands to prove your level of faith?**

# Shaniqua Rischer

## Tongual Diarrhea

*"But the people remained silent and said nothing in reply, because the king had commanded, 'Do not answer him.'"* Isaiah 36:21 NIV

I have an issue. It has blocked some of my blessings before, damaged relationships I worked hard to rebuild, and destroyed fragile experiences that otherwise would have been beautiful. It's more of a disease than an issue. The disease I have is Tongal Diarrhea (commonly known as Diarrhea of the Mouth). I talk too much, I don't know when to be quiet and leave well enough alone, and I always feel the need to explain myself/feelings (as if I need to justify what I am feeling). They say the first step is admitting you have a problem... The reason I can freely admit my...issue...is because of my Bible study group last night. I found out that the disease I have has a cure; I just need to follow it. In Isaiah 36, we come to another point in history where God does what I call an "OG" move. The Northern Kingdom of Israel has been invaded by the Assyrian armies; the people of Israel have been enslaved and taken from their land. This seemingly unbeatable power has decided that it will be the dominant ruler of all. After leaving the Northern Kingdom, the Assyrian army continues south and is now marching on Judah, the Southern Kingdom of Israel. In their dominance and invasion, they have devastated cities, taken homes, and destroyed all in their path. At the epicenter of Judah is the Lord's city, Jerusalem, which they now stand outside of waiting to conquer. It is here that God shows actions speaks louder than any words.

The Assyrian king sent his captain as an emissary to speak to Judah's king Hezekiah. The captain is brash, bold, and the words he says are enough to instantly start a fight. He went way beyond talking about "your momma"; he went to talking about "your God". He ridiculed the people, belittled their king and God, while trying his best to get them to turn on their Lord and side with the Assyrian king. He promised wealth and material goods; going so far as to say if they didn't follow the Assyrian king, the result would be them eating and drinking their own excrement and urine. Lastly, he stated that God could not stand against the Assyrian might when so many gods and nations had fallen before. Do you know what their response was? Silence. Yes, they were silent. I don't know how they did it; even now in my head I am thinking, "I wish somebody would". But they submitted to the instructions of their King and said nothing, trusting their King to deliver them.

Upon hearing all that was said, King Hezekiah went to the prophet of the Lord, Isaiah. The Lord responded and told Isaiah that this day, the Assyrian army would not harm the city or Judah further. Hezekiah was pleased and praised God. Yet, the story doesn't end there. The Assyrian king then wrote Hezekiah a letter and told him in effect, "this isn't over." He predicted he would return to rule Judah and that his God was nothing. Again, Hezekiah did not reply. Instead this time, he went directly to the temple, kneeled, laid out the letter, and prayed. He gave the situation to God and God's response was swift and on point, OG style (I encourage you to read Isaiah 36-39; it's a fascinating account). Hezekiah's response to God was to wait and praise.

In Bible study, we were asked "Where in your life can you honor God by not having a response?" So many things ran through my mind because I thought of how this year alone, my mouth has run "ahead" of God. The cure to my disorder is simple. Submit, pray and praise. I don't have to respond to everything. Sometimes, the only response God warrants of us is silence and trusting in Him to take care of the issue. Life can press us hard sometimes, people can press us to respond or they can say things to us that we badly want to respond to and shouldn't. Instead, God wants us to turn to Him. Submit to Him. Pray to Him. Praise Him. We should submit our thoughts and responses to God, going immediately to Him in prayer and simply "shut up".

**Reflection & Study Questions**

**There are times that God does require us to speak and times that He requires us to refrain from speaking. As you grow closer in your relationship Christ, you will be able to discern exactly when those times are. The key however is, are you ready to be submitted to Him and pray in all situations.**

**1. Do you suffer from "tongual diarrhea"? What can you do to solve this**

condition?

2. Where does God want you to refrain from speaking? Why do you feel He wants you to refrain?

3. What is the benefit to refraining from speaking and where in your life can you honor God by not having a response?

# The Purpose in a Dead Situation

*"Then Jesus said to them plainly, "Lazarus is dead. And I am glad for your sakes that I was not there, that you may believe. Nevertheless let us go to him." John 11:14-15 NIV*

Sometimes we want the Father to bring life to a dead situation, when we should ask why the situation died in the first place.

Once again, someone has been removed from my life...a situation has become dead. Although, I had my hand in creating the dead situation, as I navigate through the hurt and disappointment I feel, I couldn't help but ask God why this person came into my life. I had been careful who I let into my life on a personal level. I didn't ask to care for them. I didn't ask or want to get to know them. I did not want to open myself up to them; it just evolved into something deeper. Yet as I asked God that question, He made me analyze why the situation died. This is where the story of Lazarus comes in.

A dead situation doesn't have to be a friendship; it can be a job, a relationship, or any number of things in life. Sometimes, God places a dead situation in our lives because it reveals who we are, it reveals who the Lord is, and it allows us to be pruned and grow.

The dead situation in my life has truly been a learning situation. I have seen an ugly and insecure side of me, but I have also broken the stronghold of fear that I have lived with so long. Although the process was painful at times, it was also joyful. Secondly, the dead situation showed me another side of God and Christ. God has blessed me to know Him in a number of ways (i.e., Redeemer, Provider, Comforter, etc.), but I had never met Him as the Stronghold Breaker. I knew that He could do it, but I had never experienced that breaking myself. I have spoken about this before in a previous devotional (Fear or Faith), but the stronghold of fear had invaded my spirit long before I was even consciously aware. I wouldn't have known God that way if I would have never entered the situation in the first place.

Not only did I learn something in the midst of my dead situation, the other person did too. We were a blessing to each other, which admittedly, makes a dead situation harder to accept. Yet while Lazarus lay dead, Mary and Martha, his sisters, were soon to learn who Jesus really was. They were soon to witness what a blessing really looked like. Never before had a resurrection been done, but because of their dead brother, we would glimpse a portion of the glory of Christ.

Lastly, just as Mary and Martha didn't understand the purpose of Lazarus dying, their pain was a doorway to a new thing, a new purpose, and personal growth. My dead situation will be one of two things, a resurrected situation under the authority and power of Christ or it will be the doorway into a new situation. Either way, there has been a purpose in my dead situation. I believe that in full faith.

**Reflection & Study Questions**

**1. Where in your life has there been a dead situation?**

**2. Are you holding on to something dead? If so, recognize that by letting go, you will allow Christ to show you why it died in the first place.**

# Moving Without Haste

*"GO therefore and MAKE disciples of all the nations..." Matthew 28:19 NASB*

Do you know Jesus' last commandment was simply for us to GO and MAKE? He didn't give parameters to follow, He didn't tell us how to make, nor did He even tell us where to go, yet thousands of years later His life is the source of my life because somebody acted and went.

A few months back I watched the movie, Blind Side and although it was a very good movie with a feel good impression, it left me with a question that has haunted me ever since. What would my life be like if I didn't doubt, but immediately, without haste or sometimes thought, moved and acted when God told me to act? How would I have helped someone else or influenced them and/or the world? I am not talking about looking back on my life seeing regrets, missed opportunities, and asking the "what if" question either. Instead, I want to give serious consideration as to how submitted my (our) minds are to Christ. If you know me, you know that when it comes to specific areas such as my career, family, personal health, etc. that I act without hesitation and move at a moment's notice if I hear His voice. Yet in my past ministry and personal relationships, that has not always been the case. Instead, I am often seized with self-doubt.

I second guessed if I was doing or saying the right thing so much, that many times I have talked myself out of God's anointing and perfect will. Yes, God's will WILL be done, but which will is that? Do I want to live in God's perfect will or His permissive will? The answer for each of us, presumably, is His perfect will. But you cannot do that without first, knowing and recognizing His voice. We learn to distinguish His voice by spending time with Him. Once you recognize His voice, you have to stop trying to out think God. Yes, I said it. We often try to out think God (which is rooted in unbelief) and don't recognize that is what we are doing. We outthink God by focusing on a plan or the "how to" versus the "what to". We out think God by thinking our way is better and we out think God by doubting He would ever call US to do whatever task He has lead us to perform. We think surely the Master did not call such a broken, rusty, and damaged tool as ourselves; we think the Master surely didn't call a hammer to do a saw's job. Well guess what? The God we serve can. He made both the hammer and the saw. The only thing He asks is the will to do, go, make, and serve.

I am one of the most power creatures walking the planet. How do I know this? Because according to 2 Corinthians 12:9-10, His strength is made perfect in my weakness. His strength...my weakness. His strength...your weakness. What kind of life would I have if I acted and moved without haste or doubt when I heard the voice of God. I don't know, those times have past. What kind of life WILL I have when I act and move without hast or doubt when I hear the voice of God? I don't know, but I am about to find out. I invite you to recognize the power within yourself and find out too.

**Reflection & Study Questions**

**If you are facing a decision or often feel as if you can't make up your mind, I invite you to pray and submit your thoughts to God. God cannot use a double-minded person who is full of doubt.**

**1. Where do you find yourself doubting God and what was revealed?**

**2. How would your life change if you moved immediately when God instructed you to?**

**3. Why don't you move as He has instructed?**

# Forgiveness

*"As people, the very walls we construct to protect us through the years are the very walls that imprison us as we get older. They are walls of deceit, walls of omission, walls of cheating, walls of bitterness, walls of unforgiveness, walls of pride, walls of self-reliance, walls of aloofness, walls of anger, walls of absenteeism, and more." Shaniqua Rischer*

I wrote those words last week and sent them to someone. Little did I know they would come back to stare me in the face one week later. Last night, unintentionally, I hurt someone. I acted out of fear and anger and said things that are eating me up today. I thought someone's treatment of me justified what I said to them; I was going to set them straight. Although I already knew it, in the moment, it was so easy to forget that hurting people…hurt people. Even though I want this person to understand what brought me to that point and forgive me, I am not sure if they will and I have to accept that. What is harder is forgiving myself and accepting forgiveness from God because I ignored the Holy Spirit and what He was trying to tell me…show me. Right before I hurt this person with my words, I had just thanked God for my divine appointments of that day and unfortunately didn't recognize the one that was coming my way yet still. I was on a spiritual high, but even that didn't prepare me to respond in Christ to a fellow Christian. Instead, I reacted in the flesh, out of anger, hurt, and disappointment. All of which are feelings that didn't just occur, but have been building for years. My walls.

When I think back on yesterday, my divine appointments and my own personal lesson, each incident has the same theme: forgiveness and healing. I honestly believe that God can heal any wound, but in order to do so, we have to learn to give some things to Him for healing. We have to learn that forgiveness is the ultimate sacrifice. It's dirty, it's bloody, it's hard work, it's full of grace, and it's full of mercy, but it cannot be done apart from Him. As I tried to identify a scripture to use in this devotional, I couldn't. Instead, the only thing I could think about was Christ. *"God so loved the world that He gave His one and only son…"* John 3:16 is the story of that forgiveness, that love, that redemption, that restoration.

Who am I not to forgive, when I want forgiveness? Who am I not to press past my old hurts and operate in forgiveness and faith, instead of operating in fear and bitterness? So much of the hurt we cause others is a response to our own pain; we simply don't know how to respond. We are imperfect people, expecting and wanting perfection in others. Forgiveness is not only about other people, it's about us. We have to submit to God and allow God to do what He does which is to heal and protect us. Whatever it is, know that it cannot be done apart from God. Nothing we do ever can be and that is what God has been teaching us all along. Apart from Him we are helpless, but in Him we can accomplish anything, even healing...even forgiveness.

Those close to me know I am long winded in my writing, but this is the first time I wanted to say so much more, but cannot. There are so many facets to forgiveness, I literally could write dozens more about it. However with what has been said, I pray that someone understand.

*"Whoever has ears, let them hear..."Matthew 11:15*

*"But blessed are your eyes because they see, and your ears because they hear." Matthew 13:6*

**Reflection & Study Questions**

**1. Who are you struggling to forgive and what are you struggling to forgive yourself for?**

# Activate Your Faith...Activate Your Power

*Jesus Is Tested in the Wilderness: "Then Jesus was led by the Spirit into the wilderness to be tempted by the devil. After fasting forty days and forty nights, he was hungry. The tempter came to him and said, "If you are the Son of God, tell these stones to become bread." Jesus answered, "It is written: 'Man shall not live on bread alone, but on every word that comes from the mouth of God.'" Then the devil took him to the holy city and had him stand on the highest point of the temple. "If you are the Son of God," he said, "throw yourself down. For it is written: "He will command his angels concerning you, and they will lift you up in their hands, so that you will not strike your foot against a stone.' Jesus answered him, "It is also written: 'Do not put the Lord your God to the test." Again, the devil took him to a very high mountain and showed him all the kingdoms of the world and their splendor. "All this I will give you," he said, "if you will bow down and worship me." Jesus said to him, "Away from me, Satan! For it is written: "Worship the Lord your God, and serve him only." Then the devil left him, and angels came and attended him." Matthew 4:1-11 NIV*

I had brunch with some friends and one of them asked me about my previous employer. I made a controversial reply regarding my direct supervisor no longer being with the company and that I was not surprised, because I had prayed about that. What made it controversial is that I knew it (or something of the sort) would occur and had in fact told my co-workers not too long after my departure from the company that the "other shoe was going to fall". You see, I did not wish any ill will on my former employer, nor was I trying to grandstand in confidence, justify my beliefs, or say what was wrong or right. I just knew who I was...a child of the King. For months prior to my departure, I prayed one scripture daily about my situation and what I was encountering as I believed I was acting and speaking according to My Father. The scripture that was my deliverance from an unhealthy work environment was *"Do not touch my anointed ones; do my prophets no harm."* (I Chronicles 16:22). So, when I experienced a backlash from my words and actions, I prayed this scripture fervently. Months later, after I was gone, I still believed that the Lord would vindicate me because I spoke what He instructed me to speak without fear. Guess what, He did.

It would be easy for me to write about how the Lord said He would avenge His own and to leave revenge to Him. However, that is not what this

75

devotional is about. Instead, it's about how to fight temptation, how to fight the attack of the enemy, and the attack in our homes, within our families, and within ourselves. Satan tried to tempt Jesus at what he thought was His weakest, after 40 days of fasting, failing to realize the absolute power of Christ as He was fasting and praying with purpose. With every temptation and thought that Satan presented to Christ, Jesus responded *"It is written…"* In those three words, Jesus showed us how to fight the enemy, Satan; yet for some reason, we do not employee our greatest weapon as often as we should; we do not activate our faith. The greatest weapon against the enemy is God's very Word. The enemy will fall every time when we employee this method. When you speak scripture into your situation, your mind is changed and your situation is changed because you activate your faith and the very presence of God. *"God is not a man that He should lie" (Numbers 23:19)* so when you pray God's Word to Him in humility and in faith as you seek Him, He will move on your behalf. You may not know a lot of scripture, but what you do know is greater than any weapon Satan can throw at you. God's living Word is greater than any weapon Satan has. God's Word delivers, Christ's words cast out demons, and the utterances of the Holy Spirit comfort and restores. All found in scripture.

When I prayed those words, I did not know how the situation would be resolved, but I did trust God enough to know that He would. I also knew as a believer that God had instructed me to do or say the unpopular and that He would protect me. And to be honest, it was resolved in a way that at first glance seemed as if the enemy won, but did not. Nearly a year later and I can honestly say that situation is one of my proudest and humblest testimonies because I witnessed the power of God's Word and prayer in every situation. My faith activated scripture so that Satan had no choice but to flee. Just as the Cross will change your life, the Word can deliver your life. So, where do you need to activate your faith through scripture? Where do you need to tell Satan what is written? Satan hates us and does not want us to realize the full power we as believers have inherited, yet, he is only as powerful as we allow him to be. Take away his power today and speak the Word into your situation, plant the Word in your heart and mind, and activate your faith. My challenge to each of you this week is to choose a scripture that applies to a situation that you need God to move in. I challenge you to pray it every day for a week, a month, or even a year.

**Reflection & Study Questions**

**1. Can you pray it until you see God's Word made manifest in your life and then praise Him and share your testimony?**

Shaniqua Rischer

## Gratefulness

*"Rejoice always, pray without ceasing, in everything give thanks; for this is the will of God in Christ Jesus for you." 1 Thessalonians 5:16-18 NKJV*

My accountability partner and I started a spiritual fast from asking God for money. For the past 4 years, we have prayed 3 mornings a week for various things, but invariably, money is always a part of our prayers. And because of that, we have seen God do some pretty awesome things with provision from bills being paid to homes being saved; from mission trips to Africa to trips home, all the while thanking God for how He provided for us in spite of bad spending habits and the never ending list of wants and needs. However, one morning, we both became fed up with it. We are simply tired of asking God for money and simply, want to just acknowledge that we have survived some rough financial times in the past and through faith, we will survive whatever financial times the future will bring.

Gratefulness. Each day I went to work, I would meet men and women who are at the end of their ropes, literally. All are uneducated, most are unemployed and of those, even more have no income, not even unemployment benefits. They have families to support and no money to support them. For 2 days, I had 2 mothers express shame in having to be on public assistance and how they didn't want it to get to that point. But at that point they are…embarrassed. Many have made bad choices, but all are seeking help in the form of a second, third, fourth, or even fifth chance. Some are recovering addicts, ex-convicts, or simply have fallen on hard times, but in all of them, not only have I sensed a spirit of desperation, I see the spirit of resiliency that can only be of God. Although all do not know Him, God has used THEM to bless ME. I am humbled, because if not for His grace, their lives would be mine, their struggles would be mine. And for that, I am grateful. Not so much that I am not living their life, but because of the life I am living.

I won't ask when the last time you thanked God for something, because I believe, most of us do thank Him when it crosses our mind. But, do we thank Him enough?

*1 Thessalonians 5:16-18 states: "Rejoice always, pray without ceasing, in everything give thanks; for this is the will of God in Christ Jesus for you."*

Gratefulness. There is a gospel song that repeats that word over and over, talking about all the things that God has provided or done for us that results in our gratefulness. However, it is easy to forget to be grateful. Life comes fast and hard at us each day; it is easy to focus on what you do not have or what you need, instead of what you do have and what you have been given. Hurt, anger, bitterness, pride, and apathy are just some of the enemies of gratefulness too. You live those words so much that you do not realize the blessings that greet you simply by opening your eyes each morning.

*1 Thessalonians 5:16-18 states: "Rejoice always, pray without ceasing, in everything give thanks; for this is the will of God in Christ Jesus for you."*

Gratefulness. I am grateful for the struggle to pay my bills because I have money to pay them. Someone doesn't have money. I am grateful for my home with the too high electricity bill and the grass that seems to always need cutting (if I could turn grass into gas...), because someone doesn't have a home. I am grateful for a daddy that calls to check on me at the oddest hours of the day and a momma that makes me cream-of-wheat in the mornings when I call her on the way to work; because NO ONE has parents like I do (trust that!).

*1 Thessalonians 5:16-18 states: "Rejoice always, pray without ceasing, in everything give thanks; for this is the will of God in Christ Jesus for you."*

Gratefulness. I am grateful for every tear I have ever shed and every hurt I have experienced. I never thought I would write that, but I am. Those hurts and those tears have taught me how to love others, to love myself, and are currently teaching me how to receive love. They are also teaching me how to treat others as I would want someone else to treat me.

*1 Thessalonians 5:16-18 states: "Rejoice always, pray without ceasing, in everything give thanks; for this is the will of God in Christ Jesus for you."*

Gratefulness. I am grateful for my faith because there are many who don't believe as I do (some close to me) and I simply cannot fathom how they live each day without faith in Christ...in God. Life would not only be overwhelming, it would be unbearable.

*1 Thessalonians 5:16-18 states: "Rejoice always, pray without ceasing, in everything give thanks; for this is the will of God in Christ Jesus for you."*

My Lord says I should rejoice always, pray without ceasing, and in everything...in lack or in abundance...in despair or in flourishing...in hurt or in joy...in strife or in peace...that I should give thanks because it is the will of God in Christ Jesus. That one verse is the mark of spiritual maturity. Wherever you are in your journey, know that it is a journey to maturity, to wisdom, and dependence on God.

**Reflection & Study Questions**

**1. What are you grateful for today?**

**2. Do you know and believe you are exactly where you are supposed to be? Recognize and be grateful for your journey.**

## God...The Virus Destroyer

*"For though we live in the world, we do not wage war as the world does. The weapons we fight with are not the weapons of the world. On the contrary, they have divine power to demolish strongholds. We demolish arguments and every pretension that sets itself up against the knowledge of God, and we take captive every thought to make it obedient to Christ." 2 Corinthians 10:3-5 NIV*

One morning, I woke up in the spirit of fear. I was physically ill with fear; my head was hurting, my heart was racing, I hadn't slept well, and I felt emotionally bereft. All because of this fear. I am terrified of flying and the next day I am had plans to leave for a mini-vacation. You would think by now, I would be accustom to flying, but I am not. Each time, it takes an effort beyond me to actually get on the plane. To make matters worse, I had a few "near misses" that week with accidents. That Tuesday, I almost had a head on collision. The only thing that stopped me from hitting the other car as it spun out of control in front of me was the fact that for once, I wasn't speeding. Even though thankful, that incident served to only feed my fear this particular week. Every day since that near miss, I had been fearful of dying from an act of terror, malfunction, or tower error while on the plane.

That same morning, I had the unique experience of someone hacking into my work e-mail. It went well beyond a malicious virus; instead a malicious person changed the password to my email account, changed the signature, set-up a dummy account to forward/receive replies and sent an e-mail requesting money because "I" was stranded. However, the ironic thing, as I spoke with someone that received the e-mail, they said "It sounded just like you (as in tone of). Like the e-mails you normally send."

As I was telling my accountability partner everything that morning, she heard the fear in my voice and the exhaustion from being emotionally taxed. Randomly (this never happens like this for me), she opened her Bible and selected a scripture to read. The scripture she so randomly flipped to was 2 Corinthians 10:5. That should have been the first clue that God was about to speak to me. However, when it came time to pray, I asked her to go first because honestly, I was too shook up to pray. All I could feel was fear. All I could think about was the fact that bad things were happening and then she began to pray. As she prayed for me, I couldn't help, but be moved because she prayed the very words I needed to hear. God spoke to me through her about my most private thoughts this very morning. It was almost eerie because I felt loved, heard, and God's acknowledgement at the same time. In the midst of praying, she said something that blew my mind. She said God can identify and destroy any virus. Although she was praying specifically about my e-mail account at that time, she was also talking about me. You see fear is an insidious "virus" that invades, influences, and make you something you are not.

The malicious e-mail sounded like me, it came from my e-mail address, and it looked like me, but it wasn't me. Instead, it was a sad and destructive imitation of me, a copy. In the midst of her praying, it dawned on me this is exactly what my fear was doing to me. I sounded like me, I looked like me, but how I was thinking this particular week, just was not me. I was a sad and destructive copy of my very self. Has fear done the same to you? Are you behaving in a manner that is not really you all because of fear? Has fear made you so uncomfortable to be yourself because you fear rejection? Do you fear being left? Or perhaps you fear losing control (which is the root cause of my fear of flying). Insidious; that's what fear is and that is how the devil behaves. The definition says it all: "stealthily treacherous or deceitful; intended to entrap or beguile; or operating or proceeding in an inconspicuous or seemingly harmless way but actually with grave effect."

Yes, I am terrified of flying, but I do it because I no longer want to be imprisoned. I want to see God's world. That fear is real in how it manifests itself in my body, but it is not real in how it manifests itself in my spirit. My faith is simply greater than any fear. Our faith is greater than any fear. So once again, I had to take captive fear, those imaginative thoughts, and make them obedient to Christ. You must do the same. It is time to stop living the imitation of your life.

I've said it before, but the battle for our spirit starts in our mind. We must constantly capture our thoughts, our fears, our feelings of inadequacy, and the feeling that God is not enough…and place them at the cross. Christ has already born them. So why do we continue to carry them? As I looked at the definition of insidious, I wondered what words were the opposite. I read words such as **faithful, frank**, honest, **loyal**, open, sincere, **trustworthy, truthful, upright** and HOLY (my addition). All of which sounds like God.

Reflection & Study Questions

Scripture said it best, "We demolish arguments and every pretension that sets itself up against the knowledge of God". We must demolish anything that sets itself up against our knowledge of God. My knowledge of God is simple, Great Is His Mercy; Great Is His Love; Great Is His faithfulness, He is…I AM.

1. What do you know about God?

2. What is He revealing about Himself to you?

Shaniqua Rischer

### The God Balance...

*"The Lord and his disciples were traveling along and came to a village. When they got there, a woman named Martha welcomed him into her home. She had a sister named Mary, who sat down in front of the Lord and was listening to what he said. Martha was worried about all that had to be done. Finally, she went to Jesus and said, "Lord, doesn't it bother you that my sister has left me to do all the work by myself? Tell her to come and help me!" The Lord answered, "Martha, Martha! You are worried and upset about so many things, but only one thing is necessary. Mary has chosen what is best, and it will not be taken away from her." Luke 10:38-42 CEV*

Work, Family, Friends, and God. Family, Work, Friends, and God. Friends, Family, Work, and God. What's wrong with those words? They are all out of order. If you can sum up my life in one biblical character it wouldn't be Moses, Rahab, Peter, or even Paul; instead it would be Martha. Yes, Martha. As a matter of fact, I think I have Martha beat at being her. At least it feels that way sometimes.

One morning, I forgot to pray. I didn't forget to send the work email before I actually went to work. I didn't forget to check Facebook, nor did I forget to even brush my teeth (nor have I ever forgotten that), but I did forget to talk to the Father. I forgot to acknowledge His very presence in my life this morning. It's not the first time and I fervently hope it is the last. Ironically, I woke up this morning with one thought on my mind, I need a "mini-me". Although I needed a "mini-me" I am not about to miraculously receive one and I must honestly admit to myself that I can't do everything I have committed myself to doing. As it stands, sometimes my life looks like I barely have time for Him.

Upon reflection, I realized I didn't need to balance my work, ministry, and social life. Instead, I need a God balance. Specifically, I needed to stop fitting God into my life and ensure God is the center of my life at ALL times. Earlier this year I wrote about God taking my faith to a new level; well, a part of that new level has been "trimming the fat" from my life. You see, it is easy for me to add various commitments all in the form of a good cause to my life, to volunteer, to serve on this Board, to counsel a friend or stranger, but all of that is out of order if God is not my center.

In Luke, we are introduced to a woman that is the same as many, if not all, of us at one time or another. Jesus' rebuke of Martha was not meant to dishonor the work she was doing on His behalf, instead it was a reminder that her very purpose for being was sitting right before her in her own house! Jesus, the center of the universe, God's anointed sacrificial lamb, the Alpha and Omega, was in reaching distance of Martha. Yet instead of slowing down long enough to listen to His wise words, Martha chose to do the mundane tasks she thought needed to be done. We all make the same mistakes often without thought. Jesus' words to Martha then, hold true today. The Father wants our best and first fruit. He wants to be the center of our life and attention, rightfully so, and not an afterthought. Yet how many times have we read or heard that very concept, only to lapse to a life while God is secondary?

In order to achieve the God balance, we must acknowledge just how far down we have placed God in our lives. We may say He reigns and is Lord of All, but does our life and walk reflect that? Are we dedicated in prayer to Him? Do we honestly and truly seek Him in all decisions (big and small)? Do we respond to His gentle nudges or do we wait until we cry out in pain or need to seek Him? Christ is waiting to teach us how to serve Him faithfully and live a life more abundantly. Christ is waiting for us to lay our burdens, our commitments, and our priorities at His feet, not as an afterthought, but as the first thought. I can honestly say it is during those periods of time, when I first opened my eyes and started talking to the Lord and immediately fell to my knees, that I felt as if my life was in perspective. It is a time supersedes my going to the bathroom, before brushing my teeth, or reaching for the phone to see what I had missed while sleeping.

My God balance starts when I push the world out and usher myself before His throne. It is easy to become distracted with commitments, family, friends, work, or even self. Yet through Martha, you and I have learned a valuable lesson. Don't miss the Lord's presence in your life because you are too busy, even for Him.

**Reflection & Study Questions**

1. How many times per day do you pray to speak to the Lord? Be honest, do you only speak to Him when you have issue?

2. Do you honestly and truly seek Him in all decisions (big and small)? If so, give some examples.

3. Do you take time away from distractions to pray to Him or do you allow distractions to interrupt your time with God?

# The Replacement Factor

*"I am the LORD, and there is no other; apart from me there is no God. I will strengthen you, though you have not acknowledged me, so that from the rising of the sun to the place of its setting people may know there is none besides me." Isaiah 45:5-6 CEB*

*"I am the LORD, and there is no other. I have not spoken in secret, from somewhere in a land of darkness; I have not said to Jacob's descendants, 'Seek Me in vain.' I, the LORD, speak the truth; I declare what is right." Isaiah 45:18-19 CEB*

The last few weeks have been a series of fortunate events; completely random, but thought-provoking all the same. A few weeks ago I had a conversation with a man who was a self-proclaimed Agnostic. I didn't start the dialogue, but after a few minutes of hearing him share his views and beliefs with others, I felt compelled to join in the conversation. We talked and shared for more than 30minutes. He was used to Christians trying to convert him and expressed surprise that I didn't. Conversion is not my intent; instead, I pray. I addressed some of his concerns about Christianity, the relationship, not just the religion. One of his most compelling statements centered around why most people couldn't just accept life as it is. He strongly believed that science has proven religion to be obsolete, yet he couldn't explain the inherent need in humans to seek answers beyond what has already been proven. It baffled him.

Recently, I read an interesting article on climate controlled farming in the Netherlands. The premise of the article was that due to the global food crisis, more inventive ways need to be found to grow and harvest crops. Scientists have found a way to do just that by growing plants in a climate controlled, sunless, rainless environment. One scientist in the article stated that "Sunlight is not only unnecessary but can be harmful."

I have been having an ongoing dialogue with a friend of mind about sex. It is an age old debate that every person of faith will have at least once (ok, at least 10x times) in their lives. Do we listen to the Spirit or give in to the flesh? She is conflicted because her spirit and her beliefs have clearly pointed her in one way, whereas the world and her flesh are pointing to the exact opposite.

Through all of these non-similar events, thoughts, and conversations I have noticed a centralized theme. We are trying to replace God in every aspect of our lives. In my conversation with the agnostic, I realized what made him so uncomfortable was his inability to explain away that inherent voice within each of us that seeks a higher power. I am not a scientist, but from what I remember in science class, I was always told that plants needed sunlight to thrive and grow (something to do with photosynthesis). I have personally seen God's Miracle-Gro in rainwater, so surely plants need that too. Although I am not trying to minimize the scientific advancements made nor deny the food crisis, it amazed me to think that the very things the Creator has put in place to sustain us (rain, sunlight, etc.), some seek to replace and make obsolete with man-made inventions. Lastly, my friend and I both know what the Spirit tells us to do, yet we try to replace the Spirit with reasoning, creating excuses, and giving in to our flesh; ignoring the inherent voice within that seeks to lead and guide us.

God is not pleased, but nor is God surprised. In Chapter 45 of Isaiah, God repeats one thing *"He is God; there is no other."* You would think that would be easy to believe and even easier to acknowledge, but it is not. We often ignore the voice of God in our lives creating our own doubt and indecision by ignoring His word. We are constantly on this trek to seek and find God, yet God is apparent everywhere around us. So often people speak about ignoring warning signs, but what about when we ignore the God signs? The creation cannot replace the Creator, but so often we try. We cannot replace God by an idol, ideal, or thought.

So, how do we find God? How do we hear His voice and determine His Will? It would be easy for me to say to listen to that "quiet voice within", but we have been tone deaf for so long that we can't distinguish any voice...God's, our own, or the enemy's. Yet God has given us a way to discern His very Will for our lives. The Holy Bible. The Bible is literally God's road map for humanity. It's not an easy map to read, yet it covers every conceivable thought and idea by man. The Bible is a living application. Trouble with your neighbor? The Bible covers that. Trouble with your spouse? Yep, that's covered too. Trouble with your child? He even thought to cover that too. Do you get the picture? All of our problems, issues, and burdens are covered by His word. God answers the question the agnostic couldn't answer. We inherently seek Him because that's how He made us.

Why do we need the sun and the rains? Because God is the Creator and He has made His creation to work in perfect harmony and through imperfect brokenness, the cycle of life continues. And pre-marital sex? Yes, we know what the Word says about it and how we should refrain, but more importantly God told us how to resist our flesh. God's answers to our questions, just as to our prayers, are not always what we want to hear. It's hard for a child to understand the parent's "Because I said so." But in this instance, the omniscient, omnipresent, all powerful parent, God, actually knows what's best. It's just a matter of us trusting the Father enough to obey. The next time you wonder what God is saying, pick-up His instruction book to find out.

**Reflection & Study Questions**

**1. How can you learn how to obey Him? Are you ready to hear His voice and determine His Will?**

**2. What steps will you take to determine what and where God is leading?**

Shaniqua Rischer

## You Make Me Better

*"Brothers and sisters, if someone is caught in a sin, you who live by the Spirit should restore that person gently. But watch yourselves, or you also may be tempted. Carry each other's burdens, and in this way you will fulfill the law of Christ. If anyone thinks they are something when they are not, they deceive themselves. Each one should test their own actions. Then they can take pride in themselves alone, without comparing themselves to someone else, for each one should carry their own load. Nevertheless, the one who receives instruction in the word should share all good things with their instructor." Galatians 6:1-6 NIV*

I don't like correction, but then again, who does? I am not talking about correcting my speech or an answer to a question when I make a mistake, but when someone calls me out on my actions. Yet, the Bible has charged us to do just that with our fellow Christians. Last night, someone gave me a great compliment. They told me I make them better. I was flattered of course, but as I gave it further thought, I had to reflect on what about "me" makes them better. The person then went on to say, "if I am consistent enough and show you I am serious, I know you will not be as reserved with me and our friendship can grow"; in other words they would build trust with me. That simple expression made me reflect on what it means to be a friend AND what it means to be a Christian. Admitting, I am a hard friend to have; I am overly sensitive at times, indifferent/hard at other times, but also very demanding, meaning if I give you 110%, then I expect 110% back. Yet for whatever reason, to this one person, I made them better in spite of all my flaws. That is exactly what being a friend and the fellowship of Christ is about, dependability and accountability.

A previous devotional "Imposters of the Spirit" spoke about the Fruits of the Spirit and how as we mature in Christ, the Fruits of the Spirit (Galatians 5:22-23) should be apparent in ourselves and in other Christians. The challenge was for each of us to truly examine ourselves and our inner circle of family/friends in light of the Fruits of the Spirit. As we learn to exhibit the Fruits of the Spirit, there will naturally be a war between our spiritual and human selves. It's only understandable, yet when used correctly, correction from a friend or other Christians can in fact make us better. If we profess to love our friends and family as much as we do, why then do we continue to consign on a walk that is not edifying and pleasing to the Spirit?

Or, we estrange ourselves from those that are bold enough to confront us about our wrongs.

In an effort to be better followers of Christ, we should hold ourselves accountable and restore gently in correction those closest to us. This does not give us permission to go tell each and every one we may disagree with that they are going "to hell" because of the sin in their life; one because you are standing in judgment of others which God clearly speaks against and secondly, they may come running to tell you the same thing. Instead, with a sense of discernment and based on your relationship with them, show them how the Word of God wants different for them and their life. Show them how to become better.

As I stated, I don't like to be corrected, but more than that I don't want to fail the very people I profess to care about. So, I try (and sometimes fail miserably), to speak the truth in love (Ephesians 4:15) to those that enter my life because I love them that much. I love them enough to want to make them better just as they have made me better. I love them enough to show them the Fruits of the Spirit and my walk with Christ, i.e. love, joy, peace, kindness, etc. Without accountability we will have stunted growth because for many, we are not able to distinguish our voice from the enemies' voice, and from the Lord. What we see as right may very well be wrong. Therefore, do not be afraid to receive correction nor to give correction. Instead, approach correction prayerfully and with love, honor, and respect for the other's person journey. You may not just help make them better, but may become better in the process.

**Reflection & Study Questions**

**1. Are you afraid to receive correction or to give correction? Why?**

**2. What if someone never corrected you? Where would you be and what would you be doing right now?**

**3. Do you know you are accountable for your actions and you need correction? How does correction help you?**

Shaniqua Rischer

## Maturing Walk: The "I Wish Somebody Would" Moment

*"We also glory in our sufferings, because we know that suffering produces perseverance; perseverance, character; and character, hope. And hope does not put us to shame, because God's love has been poured out into our hearts through the Holy Spirit, who has been given to us." Romans 5:3-5 NIV*

*"Therefore, if anyone is in Christ, he is a new creation. The old has passed away; behold, the new has come." 2 Corinthians 5:17 KJV*

These past few weeks I have been focusing on the Fruits of the Spirits (Galatians 5:22-23), Imposters of the Spirit; how they are manifested in us and in others. I attempted to discuss how God has charged us to hold each other accountable to become better through correction; You Make Me Better (Galatians 6:1-6). Well, now God has once again used my life as a way to exhibit how the Fruits of the Spirit flow out of a maturing and submitted walk.

Have you ever had a conversation with your friends (or yourself) where you've said, "I wish somebody would (blank)!" That statement is usually followed by the thought or comment of WHAT you would do if that person actually dared to (blank). Well, I had that moment twice this week on different days. The first one was minor and resulted in my exercising self-control (I passed), but the last incident shocked even me. You see, I was told this week that I "was not going to get paid". Yes, you read that right. Due to this economy and other factors, my job notified us payroll was being suspended this week. Now normally, I would testify to how God provided (which He did), but that's not what this devotional is about. Instead, this devotional is about my response or lack of response to this news.

Now before I continue, I ask you, what's your "I wish somebody would (blank)" moment? If you are anything like me, that scenario really never crossed your mind as a possibility, but if you are also like me, you expect yourself to respond in a less than Christ-like way. When told that my company was suspending payroll, and that I was expected to keep working in spite of that delayed payment, I did the exact opposite of what I even expected of myself. I remained at peace, reacted calmly, AND even though my close friends wonder why I am still there, I didn't quit. I didn't even get "Tongual Diarrhea".

You see, I know I am where God wants me to be. I have left jobs before (without another job), but I could not leave this one because it is where God has called me to be. I am not a Saint (far from it) nor am I rich (far from that too), but my job is a ministry and I recognize that.

So, what brought out this attitude? What caused me to react in a way that is totally different than even I would have expected of myself? The answer is none other than my maturing faith and walk with God. As I walk this journey of faith and mature in Christ, I truly have come to realize just how much of a new creature in Christ I am. God's word says that "suffering produces perseverance; perseverance, character; and character, hope" and that hope is of the Holy Spirit. So are the Fruits of the Spirit: love, joy, peace, patience, kindness, goodness, faithfulness, gentleness, and self-control. All of these define the life of a maturing Christian, someone who is in the process of growing in the likeness of God.

The same can be said of you. You are a new creature in Christ, but maybe you're like me and don't recognize how new. Often, we see ourselves as others see us or accept the image we have always held of ourselves. God IS producing Fruit in our lives. Every trial, tribulation, or triumph gives testimony to His Fruit and produces more fruit. And God, being the loving and merciful father that He is, will sometimes use situations to reveal to you (as He had to do with me), the new you.

I share my personal experience not to be boastful of my Christ-like response in the face of trials; instead, I share it to be boastful of the great work that God is doing in me! He took me and made me into a better me. God did that even though I expected and thought like the old me.

## Reflection & Study Questions

**1. Are you ready to maturely walk into your destiny and fully recognize that God is changing you?**

**2. Do you understand that as long as you submit to Him you won't remain the person you were?**

**3. Are you ready to change? If not, what is holding you back?**

Shaniqua Rischer

## Empty Spirit: The Dark Night of the Soul

*"But we have this treasure in jars of clay to show that this all-surpassing power is from God and not from us." 2 Corinthians 4:7-9 NIV*

*"And we know that in all things God works for the good of those who love him, who have been called according to his purpose." Romans 8:28 NIV*

As I was reflecting on the Fruits of the Spirits (Galatians 5:22-23) and how to end this series, I began to wonder what about when life's circumstances cause the fruit to all but disappear or so it seems. What happens when you no longer have joy, are living in the absence of peace, and your longsuffering is…well, long? Years ago, in my Spiritual Formation class in "Bible College", my teacher spoke about a time in a person's life where they feel adrift and spiritually bereft called the "Dark Night of the Soul". The phrase describes spiritual discontent, disconnectedness, and a general feeling of separation from God over an extended period of time. Although it is not a biblical term and I had never heard it in any sermon before (or after), it is widely used amongst many theologians, pastors, and spiritualists. Initially, it was a hard concept for me to understand; yet upon reflection, I realize it was hard for me to understand because the concept, at the time, was foreign to me. How could I be a Christian yet feel abandoned and disconnected from God over a long period of time? Little did I know, soon thereafter I would begin the journey of my own "Dark Night of the Soul". One of the key things that I remember during class discussions was that once started and the journey complete; you would never be the same. I can attest to that. You see, it is easy to write about how our walk with Christ should produce the Fruits of the Spirit in our lives, but it is hard to understand your walk with Christ in the absence of that Fruit. It is hard to understand when you are quite honestly, empty. Many of you may not know what to call that emptiness you feel; that separation you can almost see, and sadly our churches and church leaders often ignore the occurrence of the "Dark Night of the Soul". My "Dark Night of the Soul" did not occur because of one instigating factor; instead it was the culmination of years of disappointments in God, man, and me. However, although trying, the "Dark Night of the Soul" results in greater faith and a greater intimacy with God.

So, what do you do when you encounter something that robs your Spirit of Fruit? When you are in the pit of despair and reaching out to a God whose hand you doubt is reaching back?

You keep reaching.

In my opinion, this is where many people of faith falter. They simply stop following. My "Dark Night of the Soul" lasted for over 2 years. I went to church, and although my praises felt empty, I kept praising. I prayed and no longer believed I would see the fruition of those prayers, but I kept praying. To look at me, you would see no difference in me, but I knew. I stopped writing devotionals and I withdrew from God because I thought He withdrew from me. If you are where I am describing, if you feel separation from Him, you are not alone. Great men and women of God, of Christ, have experienced the same thing and we don't share it. We don't readily share how the suffering turned into patience; we do not share how the despair turned into joy, nor how the discord turned into peace.

The journey to the Fruits of the Spirit is the Cross; the Cross we bare each and every day. In Romans, Paul wrote that in ALL things God works for good to those that love Him, in ALL things. The cross that Jesus bore worked for the good of humanity. It produced Fruit. It produced you. Wherever you are in your journey of the soul, keep reaching to Him. Keep praying to Him. Keep praising Him. Keep the faith; because on the other side you recognize the purpose in the pain, the suffering, the despair, and the separation is the sweetest Fruit you will ever have. Have you heard of the Sustaining Fruit? The Fruit of the Spirit is that love, joy, peace, patience, kindness, goodness, faithfulness, gentleness, and self-control you can experience. You will then understand "we are hard pressed on every side, but not crushed; perplexed, but not in despair; persecuted, but not abandoned; struck down, but not destroyed." 2 Corinthians 4:7-9

**Reflection & Study Questions**

**1. Have you experienced the "Dark Night of the Soul"; when you don't "feel" God, no longer have joy, are living in the absence of peace, and your longsuffering seems to be long? If so, how did you react in the midst of your journey?**

**2. What are ways that you can obtain, maintain and sustain the Sustaining Fruit?**

# For Those Who Hurt and Hunger

*"Come to Me, all you who are weary and burdened, and I will give you rest. Take My yoke upon you and learn from Me, for I am gentle and humble in heart, and you will find rest for your souls. For My yoke is easy and My burden is light." Matthew 11:28-30 NIV*

Unless I am out of town, I rarely miss attending church. Yet one day, it was hard to walk inside because sometimes, when you walk into the House of the Lord, everything that you want to hide is exposed. For me, this particular day I walked in and something about the Holy Spirit nudged my spirit and exposed all of the hurt and shame I tried to desperately bottle up. The harder I tried to maintain my composure, the harder it was for me to remain stoic. You see, when you are used to being there for everybody, it is hard to admit you need help or everything is not alright with you. Although I am pretty open with my devotionals, it is hard for me to not be reserved most of the times. I felt undone. However, when I think about one of the purposes of the church, I am reminded that the church is supposed to be a place for the broken, the sick, and all those that hurt and hunger. So, what better place to go when you're hurting and tired of hiding?

The Saturday prior to this Sunday I mentioned, I was asked; who I sought to reach with my ministry and devotionals; the answer was simple to me. I seek to reach all those who hurt and hunger. And no matter how I try to hide the ugly or shameful parts of my walk, I share because I am not the only one who struggles. It is those things we try to hide or ignore, that often fester and manifest in other parts of our life. So, if we are honest with ourselves, every one inhabiting this magnificent and fallen planet hurts and hungers. We all hurt; we all are seeking and hungry to find love, acceptance, and peace. Yet as we seek those peaceful moments, those moments of total acceptance and unconditional love, we often become dejected and tired. Weary. We are broken beings that have been patched and re-patched again and again. As we are re-patched, we often try to hide the hurt we are experiencing; deny that it has taken place. But, eventually, we can't.

In Matthew 11, Jesus is talking to each of us. He is talking to the weary; those who carry great burdens and His instructions are very clear as He states "Come to Me" for rest is with Him. One day, my best friend and accountability partner told me that here recently, I haven't been sounding as joyful as usual. She told me I usually have my moments, but always snap back. She is right. I usually snap back after 24-hours, however this time, not as quickly. I'm tired and weary. I'm tired because although I absolutely love my job and believe in the ministry I do, I no longer want to be there. Each day I feel like I am being "blind-sided" and I never know what I am walking into. I am weary because I have been on an emotional roller-coaster recently and everything I thought about myself has been questioned, not only by me, but by someone I grew to care about. Only someone you care about can cut you and you can cut only someone who cares about you. As I walked in His House on that Sunday I referred to earlier, the altar call for prayer was given, I sought prayer. Normally, I refrain from going not because I do not believe in the "power of prayer" (I am an Intercessor), but I too struggle with being "private". If I go to the alter, I am admitting I need prayer. Well, at this time I do. However, I would rather tell someone I need prayer than to suffer in silence and block His Healing Hand from moving. The Intercessor for many sought out intercession from another as I laid it at Jesus' feet.

These are trying times that we live in, but the resiliency of the Spirit cannot ever be defeated. Just when we wonder where we can go, who we can turn to, remember the house of the Lord. His desire is for us to seek Him, to come to Him, and to receive rest with Him. He is the gentleness we need, the unconditional love and acceptance we seek. On Friday morning, someone gave me a bracelet that said "God is Big enough". Yes, He is and His shoulders are wide enough. His Son has carried the cross, His burden is light. All we have to do is come.

## Reflection & Study Questions

**1. Do you feel as if you are broken and have been re-matched and are you hiding your hurt from others? If so, why do you feel hiding is necessary?**

**2. If you are hiding your hurt and weariness, have you made an effort to lay it down at the feet of Christ? Why or why not?**

**3. Keeping our burdens hinder us from living God's intended life. If**

you are carry your burdens, what life are you missing?

4. Do you find it hard to ask others for prayer? If so, why? Why does God use other people (intercessors) to pray for us?

Shaniqua Rischer

## Complete Dependence

*"Then the LORD said to Moses, 'I will rain down bread from heaven for you. The people are to go out each day and gather enough for that day. In this way I will test them and see whether they will follow my instructions.' " Exodus 16:4 NIV*

How many of you are living pay check to pay check? I am. According to CareerBuilder.com in 2010, 77% of all Americans were living pay check to pay check. This does not take into account those who are unemployed. However, despite not having an abundance of disposable income, this past year, God has shown me He is truly the Lord of Provision, Jehovah-Jireh. He has shown me what it means to truly depend on Him.

Up until this past August, whenever payday rolled around, I rarely gave thought as to whether my job would pay me for the work that I did. Just like I expected the lights to come on when I flipped on a light switch, I'd come to expect a paycheck every two weeks. But, what happens when you do a job and have to wonder if you will get paid? It's enough to make you realize that you have had faith in a system to provide your needs, when in reality it has been God who has been your provider.

These past few weeks have reminded me of the children of Israel and how alike we are. A few weeks ago, I wrote in "Maturing Walk" about being told by my employer that I would not get paid due to financial strains the organization was under. While I was ultimately paid, I've had to inquire about every paycheck since then and have lived with that same uncertainty every week. I no longer am paid via direct deposit, but instead receive a physical check in the mail that I await anxiously.

I have been laid-off before, but this is different. If I were to be laid-off, although it would be hard, I would be able to draw unemployment. Instead, I am living in a constant state of uncertainty. As I ask the Lord, "How long can I go on like this?" He answered, "as long as I have you in it." You see, much like the Israelites, I am I literally living in a wilderness situation. God delivered the nation of Israel out of bondage and slavery in Egypt, promising Israel their own "promised land". He heard the cries of His children while in bondage, remembered the promise to build a great nation, and used Moses to deliver them from Pharaoh. I have been delivered from Egypt (thankfully so), yet I am not yet at my promised land. As I am on this journey, I have become like the children of Israel. I complain, "God, why did you bring me here?" I praise Him, "God, without you I wouldn't be able to withstand this uncertainty". I have fear, "What will I do if they can't pay me next time?" Yet more than anything, I am learning a deeper meaning of depending on Him. This is one of the many lessons I have learned from this situation.

When the Children of Israel were brought out of bondage, they were faced with starvation, loss of home, and uncertainty from one day till the next. Yet, in the midst of that uncertainty, they experienced God in a new way. They received something never before seen nor seen thereafter. They received manna, the bread of life from God. Each morning, as the Israelite awoken, the very bread of Heaven, manna was waiting on them to harvest. God provided enough manna for each family and only enough for each day. They were not to keep it nor harvest more than their share. They were in complete and utter dependence upon God. They were placed in a position where they had to trust an unseen God for a seen thing. That is where I am at right now and this may be where you are, too.

Manna doesn't necessarily mean provision, it is not necessarily money. Manna can be anything that calls you to depend on Him completely. In that dependence, God wants me and you (us) to awake each morning and give whatever situation to Him. He wants us to wake in expectation of what dependence on Him provides. The Israelites were in the wilderness for 40 years. Forty years they woke up each day, depending on God to provide manna for them, to take care of their needs. Yes, during those forty years, they did complain about the manna. They complained about the wandering and wondering. Yet the focus is not on them, the focus is on God because every day, God provided.

Each of us will encounter a wilderness moment that will be a test of how we respond. My hope is that we all respond according to the magnificence of God. In that situation, there is something so beautiful and so awesome. It is the certainty of who God is. No one is greater than He. There is no dependence outside of Him. The Creator of the Heavens and Earth has called each of us to rely on Him for each and every one our needs. This means ALL of our needs. There is favor to be received in our dependence to Him. A favor that will result in something you have never seen before.

**Reflection & Study Questions**

Have you ever felt or currently feel as though you are one of the Children of Israel in a "wilderness moment"?

What areas can you focus on that you can be thankful for until He answers your prayer this area? How has your attitude been since you have been in the "wilderness"?

# Write Their Stories

*"Therefore encourage one another and build each other up, just as in fact you are doing."*
*1 Thessalonians 5:11 NIV*

*"Two are better than one, because they have a good return for their labor: If either of them falls down, one can help the other up. But pity anyone who falls and has no one to help them up. Also, if two lie down together, they will keep warm. But how can one keep warm alone? Though one may be overpowered, two can defend themselves. A cord of three strands is not quickly broken." Ecclesiastes 4:9-13 NIV*

Last week I was in a meeting and someone asked me if I planned on being at my job in a year. Although hesitant to answer, I told them I didn't know, yet the only reason I was there this long was because of my program participants; they simply inspire me to keep going. I cannot imagine leaving them at this stage because I am invested in them, their hopes and dreams. You see, what inspires and humbles me so much about my participants is their resiliency of spirit. If I was to look at my life in comparison to theirs, I would say I have been abundantly blessed. I grew up in a two parent household, I did not see the ravages of drugs or alcohol abuse in my family, my siblings and I all have degrees in higher education, and we all are successful by the world's standards. My life, although full of pit holes and trying times, in comparison to some of my participants has been a cake walk. I wonder how many of yours have been too. Yet when I look at some of them, I see a person that has been tarnished, bruised, dented, and broken. Yet I also see a spirit that has been restored, redeemed and given extra measure, extra grace, and are abundantly blessed. I see people who are daring to dream in spite of the harsh realities. I see people like "(blank)".

"(blank)" in her late 40s is unemployed. "(Blank)" lives in a half-way house, is a recovering addict, has been homeless, and is an ex-convict. "(blank)" by the world's standards should be written off. Yet "(blank)", unassuming in appearance and stature, has a vision. She wants better for her life and in spite of every stumbling block ever encountered; "(blank)" has turned her life around and is in school. As I hear stories like hers, witness individuals on the brink of giving up, I am humbled because I see how God has used them to minister to me and me to them. Friday "(blank)" entered my office with a spirit of defeat, sharing with how she needed to find a job;

her greatest fear was sleeping under the bridge again. In that moment, it became clear to me how my current predicament of Complete and Utter Dependence on Him gave me the ability to minister to her. My response to her, not as a means to trivialize her fear, was "why are you afraid of going back to what God has delivered you from before?" You see, what "(blank)", myself, and so many fail to realize is that what God did before, He can do again. "(blank)" is afraid of being homeless again. That is a very real fear and a very real possibility. But even if it comes to that, what's even more real is that God can deliver her from that…again.

I was honored to be chosen by God Friday to speak His word into "(blank's)" life and to pray for her in my office. We spoke and prayed together, I realized how her story and countless others encourage me. We are meant to encourage each other in our walks. We are meant to share our stumbling blocks, our fears, and our triumphs so that the world will come to know the Father. Every time I write a devotional, I am consumed with a feeling of nakedness and being laid bare. Yet in my transparency, this is how I minister and encourage others. We live in a society and culture where the rules of privacy are changing as everything seems to be published and made public. Yet even then, we hold back. Although I believe privacy should be honored, I also believe our testimony is what brings others to Him. You may have never lead someone to Christ the traditional way, through the story of salvation - Christ's death and resurrection for our sins, but your story can be the doorway to someone's salvation. Although I never gave you "(blank's)" name, my guess is that you pass by them every day. We are surrounded daily by someone who needs a word of encouragement. If you are not the person to share and encourage someone, someone may be the one called to encourage you. Look for those moments this week and walk with Him.

**Reflection & Study Questions**

**1. We all need encouragement. How can you encourage others?**

**2. How can you begin to pray for others more than yourself? Write a list of people in your circle and how you can pray for them.**

**3. Do you understand acts and gains of making an unselfish prayer? When someone else is delivered from a situation, you can be delivered from yours just by being obedient.**

# With Obedience Comes Sacrifice

*"Peter and the other apostles replied: "We must obey God rather than human beings! The God of our ancestors raised Jesus from the dead—whom you killed by hanging him on a cross. God exalted him to his own right hand as Prince and Savior that he might bring Israel to repentance and forgive their sins. We are witnesses of these things, and so is the Holy Spirit, whom God has given to those who obey him.' When they heard this, they were furious and wanted to put them to death."* Acts 5:29-33 NLT

Recently, during my Bible study, I came across this passage and it gave me pause because I remembered once upon a time when I cared more about obeying or pleasing man, more than God.

When I first felt God's calling on my life to ministry in a more public manner nearly seven years ago, I experienced a mental meltdown. Although, I wasn't as out there in the world as some, I was far enough where I didn't want to give up my lifestyle. I didn't want to stop partying, I didn't want to stop cussing, I didn't want to simply share my faith outside of what I normally would do, but more importantly I didn't want people to know I was even called to ministry because of my preconceived notions of what that meant. I thought, "What would they say?" You see, I knew that with obedience comes sacrifice. By living for God, I would be sacrificing my life as I knew it. Do you remember a similar time in your life? Perhaps you are there now? As I matured in Christ, I realized how that was a sign of immaturity; I was more focused on self and "man" than I was on God. I realized that the life I was trying to preserve wasn't really life at all.

"But Peter and the other apostles answered and said: "We ought to obey God rather than men."

Ironically, these words were spoken by Peter, as he stood on trial for preaching and teaching that Jesus was the Christ, the promised Messiah, for the nation of Israel before a council of Jewish leaders and judges. This was the same Peter who once stood before this very same council of men and denied Jesus. However, months later, something had changed so drastically in Peter's thinking that he went from denying the Savior to obeying Him.

What changed? He encountered the risen Savior and it changed the direction of his life; the direction of history. Knowing Jesus before the cross changed Peter into a better man; encountering Jesus after the Resurrection transformed Peter into a bold believer who was willing to be beaten or even die rather than to deny Christ again. As Christians, we are called to be transformed from out former selves into new creatures and I will be the first to admit it is hard. You live your entire life one way, only to wake up and find out how misguided, blind, and just plain stupid you sometimes were. There will be things of our prior selves that will die and although with obedience comes sacrifice, with obedience comes life. I can attest to that.

When I started this online ministry and journey with Great Is, I had grandiose visions. And although things have not turned out as I expected, I am simply humbled how God has given me more opportunities to serve Him through the sharing of my faith. Writing these devotionals may not only help you see God in another way, they help me. My obedience has been my reward because although trying at times, I have gained peace beyond what I could have ever thought possible. I see the joy and peace I am able to give people through my personal testimony. With my obedience, I no longer recognize the sacrifice because there is no sacrifice. When I look at my friends that have children, I once wondered about the life they have given up, i.e. there "me" time or the ability to just "go" when they wanted. Although an adjustment to them (and me as a friend), I recognized they have gained so much more in the process when I see their children give them unconditional love and the smiles that light up an entire room when their parents walk in the door. Such is our walk with Christ; it is easy to look at the rules and expectations of man, but true living comes through obedience and submission to the true giver of life. At least, that is what I am starting to learn. It only took me nearly 7 years to yield to Him and find out. My sincere prayer for you is wherever God is leading you, whatever you are supposed to be doing, you will lose the life you know, but will gain more than you ever imagined through obedience. My Pastor once said that "God can't give you the greatest, if you won't leave good alone."

**Reflection & Study Questions**

**1. Today is a good day to practice obedience and walk into greatness. How can you give greatly in order to receive greatly?**

## Pray the Devil Back To Hell: The Power of Prayer In Jesus' Name

*"He [Jesus] replied, 'Because you have so little faith. Truly I tell you, if you have faith as small as a mustard seed, you can say to this mountain, 'Move from here to there,' and it will move. Nothing will be impossible for you.' " Matthew 17:20 NIV*

*"Then Peter said, 'Silver or gold I do not have, but what I do have I give you. In the name of Jesus Christ of Nazareth, walk.' Taking him by the right hand, he helped him up, and instantly the man's feet and ankles became strong." Acts 3:6-7 NIV*

*"There he found a man named Aeneas, who was paralyzed and had been bedridden for eight years. 'Aeneas,' Peter said to him, 'Jesus Christ heals you. Get up and roll up your mat.' Immediately Aeneas got up." Acts 9:33-34 NIV*

God has been sending messages of confirmation to my life these past few weeks. I have being hearing His word in triplicate; during my Bible study, at church, and during my personal quiet time with Him. This week, He spoke to my spirit about the miraculous power of prayer. On this one particular evening, I watched a documentary on the Liberian peace movement titled "Praying the devil back to Hell". Those words transcended my mind, penetrated heart, and filled my spirit. You see, sometimes I wonder why I pray because it feels as if my prayers are ineffective. Now, before I go on, I do understand that sometimes God answers a prayer through silence or not acting/moving within a situation. However, as I was studying the scriptures about the disciples and the growth of the Christian church after Jesus' ascension I began to question the difference between the prayer life of those early Christians and myself. Although Peter walked with Jesus and talked with Jesus, he was filled with the same Holy Spirit that I am filled with. And with that Spirit, comes the power and authority of Christ Jesus. Last week's devotional ("With Obedience Comes Sacrifice"), discussed how Peter's life was marked by a "before and after". Prior to the crucifixion, Peter did not have the faith to cast out demons; but afterwards, in the name of Jesus, he prayed a lame man to walk, a paralyzed man to move and a dead woman to arise. What mighty works were done in Jesus' name! And how do I tap into that power? God is still in the miracle making business contrary to popular belief, so I know that the possibility is there. Jesus gave us the key to praying in all power and authority and that key is called faith, believing without doubt.

Shaniqua Rischer

I know I have seen evidence in the power of my prayers, but I am at the point in my life that I want to pray the devil back to hell. In order to do so, I have to know and believe that I actually can. I have to believe in that the power and authority of Christ resides in me through the Holy Spirit. Do you want to know how to revitalize your prayer life? You must first believe that your prayers are not just petitions to God that you hope He will answer. Instead, you most believe that what you pray, <u>according to His will</u>, is full of the absolute power and authority of Christ. So, I am asking each of you to take a challenge with me this week. My challenge is for you to do as Jesus instructed His disciples. He told them to simply believe that your prayers can move mountains. Believe that your prayers can heal someone. Believe your prayers can break an addiction. Believe your prayers can open one door and close another. What would happen if we all prayed in Jesus' name without wavering or doubt? I am ready to find out. If Jesus said it, then I believe it. His name is so powerful that demons fear it, so where do you need to invoke the name of Jesus in your life? Peter was able to heal and walk in the authority of Christ because He witnessed firsthand the life of Christ. Well, guess what? You are also a living witness to Christ's resurrection. You may not have lived a multitude of years ago when Christ walked this earth, but by your very life you are a testimony of the living Christ. The Holy Spirit confirms that in each of us, so don't doubt, but believe that our prayers can pray the devil back to hell.

**Reflection & Study Questions**

**1. Are willing to take the prayer challenge? I am not asking you to pray a certain prayer or even at a certain time. I am asking you to believe like you never have before; to ask in the authority you may not have ever realized you had, and to expect that your prayers will be answered. Pray without ceasing, pray in expectancy, and pray that His will be done. Can you do this? And do this with an open and honest with Him and yourself?**

**2. When will you start?**

# Character Flaws

*"I, therefore, the prisoner of the Lord, beseech you to walk worthy of the calling with which you were called" Ephesians 4:1 NKJV*

As I sat in Sunday Worship Service, the guest minister made a statement that I felt was very descriptive of many Christian's walks, including my own. She stated "Your character can't keep you where your anointing is taking you". Initially, I thought, "Ouch", but at the same time, I didn't think the statement applied to me. Yet when I came across this verse in Ephesians today, I had to reassess my opinion. How often do we as Christians want to go to a new level in our lives, but in reality our very character is not where it is supposed to be according to God's anointing?

For example, when was the last time you lied? Yes, even a tiny white lie. You know, when you said you were going to do something, but knew that you weren't. Or how about, the last time you cheated? No, not cheated on your spouse? Although this may also apply to this, but on your taxes or on the diet you and your friends have agreed to follow. People tend to begin to think "what they don't know won't hurt them, right?" What about the last time you turned your back on someone that needed you, i.e. a homeless person, a stranger whose car was broke down, someone that needed just $3.00 for a gallon of gas or even a friend when you didn't want to be bothered? Or what about, dare I ask, when you hedged your bets in a situation, depending more on you than God? I am guilty of some form of all of those. I've lied, I've cheated, I've turned my back on someone, AND I am guilty of depending on me...often.

Each of these, even in their smallest form, present character flaws that prohibit us from walking worthy of the life God has called us to live. And I am tired of living marginally in my walk; aren't you? I am not talking about marginally financially or even faith wise. God has called ME to a specific thing and if I am honest, I am living marginally according to that calling. There are still places in my character that are not at the level of my anointing. If I believe His Word (and I do), then each of us were created for a specific purpose. That "purpose" requires our character to be reshaped and refined according to His calling. Paul has told us that as Christians we should walk worthy of the calling God has for us. This means we should be mindful of our actions and words, focus on what it means to walk worthy of that calling and to behave accordingly. That may mean being greater in our faith walk, exhibiting trust in all things, taking a risk and stepping out on faith, or learning true submission to Him. Our walk should not be reflective of a divided mind. Instead we should be walking worthy of our calling as followers of Christ.

I know that we are human and will never be perfect. I know that we are all works in progress and will be continually called to new levels of growth; yet here recently I have had to ask myself some hard questions. Am I truly living the life God has ordained for me and if not, why not? I invite you to ask the same question of yourself.

Let's walk this journey together with Him.

**Reflection & Study Questions**

**1. Have you recognized your own character flaws?**

**2. What are they and how can you overcome and learn from them?**

## Seven Years

*"This means that anyone who belongs to Christ has become a new person. The old life is gone; a new life has begun!" 2 Corinthians 5:17 NLT*

*"Jesus turned and said to Peter, "Get behind me, Satan! You are a stumbling block to me; you do not have in mind the concerns of God, but merely human concerns." Then Jesus said to his disciples, "If any of you wants to be my follower, you must turn from your selfish ways, take up your cross, and follow me. If you try to hang on to your life, you will lose it. But if you give up your life for my sake, you will save it. And what do you benefit if you gain the whole world but lose your own soul? Is anything worth more than your soul? For the Son of Man will come with his angels in the glory of his Father and will judge all people according to their deeds." Matthew 16:23-27 NLT*

After nearly seven years of running, seven years of trying to hide it, seven years of trying to compromise, and seven years of circumventing my calling, I finally admitted to myself and my pastor Thursday that I was called to be a preacher. Seven years. During our conversation, my Pastor asked me the one question I had tried to avoid for years, "what am I afraid of?" You see, over the past seven years, I have had the same conversation with my Pastor several times. I have been trying to do God's work without the title and responsibility of preacher. When it came time to accepting and owning my calling, I never could say the words; therefore I always had an out or as some may call it, an excuse. Well, I finally said them and as I did I felt many things; joy, peace, and regret. Regret. I felt regret because I wondered what would my life have been like if I had accepted my calling all of those years ago instead of trying to hold on to a life I thought would make me happy. I felt regret because I wondered whose blessing have I blocked due to my disobedience. I felt regret as I realized I was more committed to "stuff" than to Him. I felt regret because as I spoke to my Pastor and said the words aloud, I realized how my desire for a fun and responsibility-free life, negated the privileged anointing that has been placed on my life.

When Jesus rebuked Peter it was a rebuttal to a wayward child, a child that wanted to hold on to life as he knew. As Jesus pointed out, we simply cannot. None of Christ's followers can hold on to even an ounce of our former selves. So, I am determined to move forward and give up my life for His sake. I was willing to receive my Masters in Christian Education, but I was not willing to do more than that. Ironically, as much as I love the Lord and am in love with the Lord I loved my life and my freedom more. That is a very hard thing to admit, but I can. I loved hanging out with friends, instead of doing the ministry I was called to do. I loved sleeping in more than waking up early to spend quiet time with Him. I loved my life. Yet, my life was killing me and my spirit. It was killing me not because I was doing anything "bad", but because I wasn't living as He created me to be. The sense of dissatisfaction has been growing in me because I know I was created to do more, live more, say more, and do more for His kingdom. I do not know what tomorrow brings for me now that I am embracing and accepting my calling (other than my starting the process to become a minister - pray for me). I do know I must do it and I must preach and teach the gospel. So, I ask you, what has God created you to do that you are not willing to do? Each person that inhabits this planet was born for a specific purpose. Although the will and plan of God will not be circumvented by our disobedience, our disobedience directly affects the manifestation of His will. If you don't give your life for Christ to use, who will?

I did not lose my life Thursday, I finally started to live. I did not lose myself; instead, I finally found me. The whole me. Whatever God has called you to do, my hope is that one day you will have the courage to lose yourself and do it. I may have seven years of regret, but I will not have ten. My prayer is that you will not either.

**Reflection & Study Questions**

**Each of us has a God-design purpose that speaks to our heart, our mind, and our spirit. If ignored, often find ourselves frustrated, bored, and unfulfilled.**

**1. Have you sought Him to gain understanding of your purpose?**

**2. Do you know your purpose and have not begun the step to fulfill it?**

**3. What steps can you take to identifying your purpose and implementing your vision for your life?**

# See Yourself In The Future

*"For you created my inmost being; you knit me together in my mother's womb. I praise you because I am fearfully and wonderfully made; your works are wonderful, I know that full well. My frame was not hidden from you when I was made in the secret place, when I was woven together in the depths of the earth. Your eyes saw my unformed body; all the days ordained for me were written in your book before one of them came to be." Psalm 139:13-16 NIV*

*"Jesus replied, "Blessed are you, Simon son of Jonah, for this was not revealed to you by flesh and blood, but by my Father in Heaven. And I tell you that you are Peter....I will give you the keys of the kingdom of Heaven; whatever you bind on earth will be bound in Heaven, and whatever you loose on earth will be loosed in Heaven." Matthew 16:17-19 NIV*

How many of you are waiting on God for something in your life? Are you waiting to see a promise come to fruition? I know I am. In the devotional "Seven Years", I announced my call to ministry and spoke about how I had been side-stepping the call God had on my life. One of the things that calmed my spirit after finally accepting my calling was a song by Donald Lawrence, "You are an Heir". In the song, there is a line that says we should "see ourselves in the future". What future is he speaking of? He is speaking of the future that God has for you.

Last year at this time, my friend and I were out shopping. While shopping, we saw these beautiful cupcake tea light holders that we thought would be a wonderful gift for a baby shower. So, we bought about 20 of them, all that the store had in stock. We bought them for her baby shower, even though she was not pregnant. As we stood in the store, discussing the wonderful shower for a yet imagined child, my friend made me swear not to tell anyone we were purchasing them (she gave permission for this devotional). You see, she and her husband wanted children, but thus far they did not have any. I challenged her then as I am about to challenge you now: See yourself in the future.

Scripture tells us that God is all-knowing (Omniscient) and in that He also knows us before we were formed in our mother's womb. Therefore He knew our success, He knew our failures, He knew our joys and even our despairs. In that knowledge, He invites us to often see ourselves as He sees us. He wants us to recognize and embrace our future selves. That's what I am doing now. If I was to focus on what I think a minister is (notice I said "I think" and this is not necessarily what God has said) and what I actually am, I will never move forward. Instead I am learning that I need to see myself in the future.

One of the greatest testaments of scripture to me is the life of Peter. Jesus first told Peter in Matthew 16 how He would one day transform and use Peter to build the kingdom of Heaven. Jesus told Peter his role even before Peter would deny Jesus. Yet, by Christ telling Peter then, he prepared Peter for the future that was before him. Jesus invited Peter to see himself in the future. What our Heavenly Father did then, He does today. God is inviting you to start your journey by seeing yourself in the future.

Well, it has been a year since that faithful day in the store when we bought the tea lights and after many months of praying and waiting, we had a "Sweetest Things" Baby Shower. My friend gave birth to her daughter exactly 8 days ago. You see she became pregnant 3 months after that day in the store. While standing in that store, my friend exhibited hope in her future; she stepped out on faith believing God would answer her prayers. He did. Yet just as Peter never knew and as we ourselves don't know, sometimes the first step of living the life that God has for us is seeing ourselves in the future.

**Reflection & Study Questions**

**While waiting, God wants you to exhibit faith. Faith by volunteering, seeking counseling, praying more, reading a book, or practicing patience – all to prepare you for what is in store next.**

**1. Are you waiting on God to do something great or small in your life? Are you waiting to see a promise come to fruition?**

**2. If so, what are you doing while you are waiting?**

## Our Faith: Earned Through Blood, Sweat and Tears

*"By faith Noah, when warned about things not yet seen, in holy fear built an ark to save his family. By his faith he condemned the world and became heir of the righteousness that is in keeping with faith. By faith Abraham, when called to go to a place he would later receive as his inheritance, obeyed and went, even though he did not know where he was going. And by faith even Sarah, who was past childbearing age, was enabled to bear children because she considered him faithful who had made the promise" Hebrews 11:7-12 NIV*

Sometimes, God wakes me up from a good sleep with scriptures filling my head or a word from Him that He wants me to share. This week wasn't any different, yet what I find ironic is how God keeps speaking to me in what I call surround sound. I hear His message over and over again in various formats, be it Him speaking to me or in a confirming word from someone else. So, it was no surprise to me that the very scripture and word He gave me to write about, would be the Scripture I read today in my Bible study.

I have tried to be as open about my faith and struggles as I can through these devotionals. The premise for my writing them is to show you that you are not alone and to encourage you as God has used others to encourage me. My walk, my faith, has evolved through various highs and lows. One of those highs and lows has been my job. These past few weeks I have had a few people inquire if it has gotten better and I am glad to say that it has gotten better, things are improving. However, the greatest improvement has not been in my job, but in me. When I was awakened early than I normally would awake this week, God place in my spirit the cost of faith and how it is earned. You see, my faith has been earned through blood, sweat and tears. I am speaking in literal terms. I learned that God could heal by the issues I experienced in my body. I learned God could mend a broken heart by the tears I have shed. I learned that I can change and become a different person physically though the sweat that was produced when I pushed myself beyond my own physical limitation. Yet as God showed me how my faith was earned, He took me to Hebrews to see how some of the most famous people in the Bible earned theirs.

Hebrews 11, the faith roll call, is one of the most widely known chapters in the New Testament. In Hebrews, the author gives a roll call of those biblical giants that exhibited great faith. Yet as I looked at each person, I saw the same attributes in all of them. The more they suffered, the more their faith grew. Faith was not something that easily occurred and often times, it grew out of suffering or difficult moments. Abraham left all he knew to forge a legacy for he and his family based on the instruction of God. Although the Bible doesn't talk about it in depth, I believe that Noah suffered ridicule from his neighbors as he built an ark for rain that had not yet come. Ridicule for believing in what was to come, but was not yet seen. Sarah, Abraham's wife suffered too. Being a nearly 100 year old barren woman, Sarah was regulated to being a failure in the eyes of all, even herself, because of her inability to conceive. Each of these people listed in the roll call of faith, suffered greatly for their faith. They dealt with loneliness, ridicule, and at times being thought of as a failure. Their faith was born of blood, sweat, and tears; as is your faith and as is mine. If there is one thing I have learned is that there are blessings still to be had, faith to be earned, and even suffering to overcome. So, as you reflect on your life think back on all the tests you've passed or even failed that had added to your faith badge. You have earned it. Your name may not be listed in the book of Hebrews, but for those that know Christ, it is listed in the Book of Life. Stay faithful!

**Reflection & Study Questions**

**1. During your personal time of suffering or when someone close to you is suffering, how can you stay strong and be faithful to God?**

**2. What lessons can you pass onto to someone else?**

## The Willing You…The Willing Me

*"Then I heard the voice of the Lord saying, "Whom shall I send? And who will go for us?" And I said, "Here am I. Send me!" Isaiah 6:8 NIV*

This past year has been a year of exploration for me. I've gained valuable insight into the person I am and the person I would like to become. A part of that was a conscious decision of mine to become more available for God to use. You see, I am extremely sensitive and my feelings are easily hurt by those I care about (although most never know it). I am passionate about everything and I fight for what I believe in and who I care for. Yet it's very tiring and to be honest, I had prayed before for God to cut my ability to care so much. Yes, I have prayed to God for me NOT to love. That may sound silly, but when you have a large capacity for love, you also have a greater capacity for hurt. However, before starting this ministry, Great Is, God spoke to me about my heart. He required 100%. I could not effectively minister to His children if I sought to close off a part of the very thing that blesses others. So, instead of praying not to feel love, I now pray to show love the best way I can to all I can. But that's me; what about you? Where does God desire you to be more willing? Does He want you to sing? Does He want you to welcome His children in His house? Does He want you to go talk to strangers or to give more of your financial resources? Before God can use us to the fullest, we have to be willing to be used.

In this scripture, Isaiah has encountered the Most High God and realizes how far from the holiness of God he is. As Isaiah recognizes this, he hears God ask "whom shall I send?" and his immediate response was "Here I am! Send me." God knew the shortcomings of Isaiah, but wanted to use him anyway. Isaiah knew his own shortcomings, but was willing to be used. And from his willingness, we are blessed even today. God wants your willingness. He WANTS to use you; yes, even broken, damaged, insecure you. You see, being used is not about doing something in your power; it is about God using you to do something in His power. God desires to use us to our fullest ability. Being willing causes us to stretch and grow; we will be tested, grow weary and even hurt at times, but the reward is unlike anything seen on earth…only in Heaven.

Shaniqua Rischer

**Reflection & Study Questions**

Give one of the greatest gifts before and during Christmas. That is sharing the story of the birth of Jesus Christ, our Savior. If you haven't had a chance to tell someone the true meaning of Christmas it is not too late. You can give the gift of Christ any day of the year.

1. Are you willing to share your faith with others? What is holding you back?

# God Is Faithful

*"I desire steadfast love and not sacrifice, the knowledge of God rather than burnt offerings."* Hosea 6:6 ESV

*"I'd rather for you to be faithful and to know Me than to offer sacrifices."* Hosea 6:6 CEV

I like football, but to be honest I know nothing about it. I don't know stats and understand the game haphazardly. However, in spite of that, I watched a game because I do enjoy it. So, it's ironic that as I typed this, I just saw the end to the Steelers and Broncos game where Tim Tebow threw the ball for a touchdown in the first play of overtime to win the game and ensure the Broncos advancement in the play-offs. I am not a Tebow fan as a quarterback, because again, I don't know enough about football to critique him, but as a Christian, I find myself standing with Tebow. You see, he has withstood a lot of criticism from Christians and non-Christians alike for his blatant worship and praise of OUR God and Lord on the field and off. So, as I sat down to finish writing today's devotional I saw that play and God spoke to me the same word He has been speaking to me these past few weeks. Faithful. God is faithful to us. Even when man can't understand how the impossible may happen or how we are abound in grace, those that truly know the Lord understand. God is so much more faithful to us than we are to Him. He never fails. He often surprises and He will leave your enemies and your haters, speechless. Just as God is faithful to us, He desires our faithfulness to Him. God desires us.

The scripture above says just that. Just like Israel, many of us have turned away from God to serve false idols and masters. We have committed sexual sins, behaved as prostitutes, murderers and adulterers; liars and cheaters. Our actions have proven unfaithfulness to a faithful God. Yet in spite of that, God desires us. God shows unconditional love and faithfulness to us and desires that love back. When we unashamedly give our faithful love and adoration to Him, our faithfulness is rewarded. You don't have to be a Tebow fan to understand what you are witnessing in his life. You are witnessing the manifestation of God's favor in one of His faithful children.

Shaniqua Rischer

How many of you are faithful to God? Do you stand before crowds and proclaim Him in spite of ridicule? Is your faith such a part of you, that people see Christ in you more times than not? In spite of hardships and disappointments, do you recognize and act like God still sits on the throne? In the book of Hosea, God called Hosea to show his faithfulness by marrying a prostitute, Gomer. And Hosea so loved God, that he did. He honored God through obedience and suffered ridicule because of it.

**Reflection & Study Questions**

**Have you ever asked God what He wants? I know before this day, I never had. Yes, I have told God repeatedly that I want what He wants, but it never dawned on me to ask exactly what that desire is. More than any sacrifice I could give Him, God desires my faithfulness to Him. He desires our faithfulness, in spite of ridicule, behind closed doors or even upon a public stage. As we recommit to living our lives this year, I urge each of you to live as faithful to God as He has always been to us. He not only desires it, He deserves it.**

# Chapter 4: Liberation – Why I Do What I Do! / Is It Fear or Faith?

### Why I Do What I Do?

*"But God demonstrates his own love for us in this: While we were still sinners, Christ died for us." Romans 5:8 NIV*

Do you ever wonder why I do what I do--tell you my business, pray for you and try to encourage you through my devotionals?

Some might think it's so that I can walk someone through the Romans Road for salvation and tell how Christ died for us while we were yet sinners, so we could have eternal life. While it's a great guess, and I can do that easily, to be honest with you, that's not my motivation.

The real answer is that I do it because I feel indebted for all that I am, all that I have and from where I came. I would not be the person I am if I didn't want you to also live with the peace and assurance that I live with (through good times and bad), or to receive the same overwhelming blessings that I receive, or to witness the freedom of living in Christ instead of the chains of this world.

I really feel like I owe it to you to tell you about His goodness. It amazes me every day. And I certainly owe it to Christ to share His sacrifice for us; it humbles me every moment.

I owe it.

*I owe it to tell how when I don't think I can make it, how Christ gives me strength. (Philippians 4:10)*

*I owe it to you to tell you how when it looked as if my back was against the wall, that God literally made a way out of no way, much like He did the Israelites. (Exodus 14:21)*

*I owe it to tell you how I lived in pain for so long, but then learned how Jesus is a healer. (Mark 5:25-34)*

I don't want you to be like me, but I do want you to have peace with me. Although I am an ordinary person, I am living an extraordinary life because of my own personal relationship with Christ and it is because of this that I owe you my story because it's His story. My life is the story of Christ. Each thing that He does for us, how He saves and redeems, is just one more miracle being written in the book of life. If the Bible were still being written, my life would be reflected as one of the miracles of Christ and so would each of yours. How do I know it? Because the same miracles He did then, He is doing today. He is the living Word. He is God.

So the next time you meet someone, consider the debt you owe to them and to Him. Our testimonies are not our own, but tools as well. Just as the word of God is a two-edge sword, so are our lives; one side to grow us and one side to help grow someone else. So be the face of Christ. It may be cliché, but truly you may be the only Bible they ever read.

**Reflection & Study Questions**

**1. Do you ever wonder some give their testimonies so freely?**

**2. Do you have faith in Christ to turn your tests into testimonies?**

**3. How can you share your testimony and walk Christ with someone else?**

**Trust Him enough for you to be open with others to assist them in their areas of weakness.**

## An Exercise in Trust

*"Therefore take no thought, saying, 'What shall we eat?' or 'What shall we drink?' or 'Wherewith shall we be clothed?' (For after all these things do the Gentiles seek.) For your Heavenly Father knoweth that ye have need of all these things. But seek ye first the Kingdom of God and His righteousness, and all these things shall be added unto you. "Take therefore no thought for the morrow, for the morrow shall take thought for the things of itself. Sufficient unto the day is the evil thereof." Matthew 6:31-34 KJV*

By the time some of you read this, I will be on a plane to the Gambia, a small country in West Africa. I am the team leader for a mission group from my church and was given the opportunity because I told my Pastor about my hopes for my non-profit, "At the Cross Global Ministries", to give people the opportunity to share the gospel via missions and other avenues. Additionally, later this year, I am supposed to return to Africa for another mission trip to Ghana. One is a trip I had verbally committed to attend last year prior to my leaving my job (and tried to back out of after leaving my job until I was told I was not exhibiting faith), the other is an opportunity I did not see coming. Neither, were truly a part of my plans on January 1, 2012. Neither was being unemployed. Half way through the year, I must ask you, is your life going as planned? Because mine isn't!

For the first time in my life, I can honestly say I don't have any plans for my future. I have hopes for some things, such as my ministry for next year, but right now that seems a dream I have been spinning my wheels on because even that has not gone as I planned. Yet beyond my dream of ministry, nothing. There is nothing occurring in my life to give me a glimpse into what my future holds. Most people employed know what they will be doing today, they will be at work. Those with family assume they will see their family this evening and the next and the next. I understand that we don't know what may happen in the future, tragedy can occur at any time, but most still have an idea of a plan for their future. Yet, in a real since, I do not have those plans. Not like I used to; I am literally living my life day by day...in the dark.

*Seek ye first the Kingdom of God...*

This space is new to me, because I plan, organize, and [over] analyze everything; I do not know how to live in the moment because I am already thinking, planning and anticipating the next. But this space I am in is obviously what God wants because it has created total dependence on Him. It has caused me to seek Him first.

Many of us are living life out of the order that God told us we should live. In Matthew, Jesus gives us that order. Seek the Kingdom first and God will add the rest. In our culture, we seek to add the rest and then ask God to join the party. We make grandiose plans or think our life will be one way, when scripture clearly tells us that God should order our steps (Proverbs 16:9) and delights in every detail of our life. (Psalm 37:23) We are even admonished in James 4:13-16 about making our own plans because we are relying on self and not God.

*Seek ye first the Kingdom of God…*

So why do we do the opposite? Why do we focus on what we can obtain versus what God gives us? Sadly, it all comes down to trust. We trust ourselves to provide versus trusting the Lord to give. I am not just talking about material wealth either. We are so self-sufficient we leave God out of our life equation when God IS the equation. He desires to show us His plans and not our showing Him our plans.

*Seek ye first the Kingdom of God…*

This is a lesson I obviously am in the midst of learning. Just as I get one lesson learned, God shows me infinite more. As He is revealing my life to me, I am learning so many other lessons as well. I am learning humility because you have to be humble to accept from someone what you used to be able to buy for yourself. I am learning about giving more grace and mercy for others (learned that last week as a matter of fact) because it is being given to me. I am learning how to be broken before others. These are the true things that God wants to add to each of us. The rest, the material goods and even the food we eat and shelter we seek, are all by-products of His giving.

Nothing is going as I have planned this year, but everything is going as He planned – thankfully so. I have been abundantly blessed beyond measure. I couldn't have planned this year if I tried (my thinking is too finite and structured –in the box- for that). So, what plans do you have for your life tomorrow? Regardless of what they may be, start off by seeking Him first. Ask Him what He wants for your life. After all, He is your creator.

**Reflection & Study Questions**

**1. What experience have you had that may have caused you may not have trusted God?**

**2. What were and are your steps to be able to trust in Him more in the future?**

Shaniqua Rischer

## Up For Debate – The Word of God

*"For my thoughts are not your thoughts, neither are your ways my ways,' declares the Lord. 'As the Heavens are higher than the earth, so are my ways higher than your ways and my thoughts than your thoughts. As the rain and the snow come down from Heaven, and do not return to it without watering the earth and making it bud and flourish, so that it yields seed for the sower and bread for the eater, so is my word that goes out from my mouth: It will not return to me empty, but will accomplish what I desire and achieve the purpose for which I sent it." Isaiah 55:8-10 NIV*

Why is Christianity the only religion where people debate the Word of God? To my knowledge, no one really says Buddha meant this or Muhammad was talking about this when they speak of their sacred texts, but people always are about interpreting the Bible and either manipulating it for their purposes or trying to bend it to current times. Yet, the interesting thing is that people make their "arguments" from an intelligent standpoint, a point of reason. Well, if there is one thing I have learned is that although God is a God of design and order, He is not a God of human reason. Why? Because our thoughts are not His thoughts, our ways are not His ways. As much as we try to disagree or find a better way, God's word still stands without adulteration (to debase or make impure by adding inferior materials or elements); it stands even without interpretation or understanding.

For those that know me, you probably have realized that one of my biggest stumbling blocks is my desire and attempt to understand everything. In order for me to trust it, I have to understand it. In order for me to believe it, I have to understand it. And originally in order for me to have faith, I used to have to see it. That is not how God works even though we like to box Him into our thinking.

As Christians, we are called to be the salt of the earth and in our culture it is getting harder and harder to be so. Not because we falter in our walk (which we all do), but because our culture is so pervasive. Our sense of right and wrong, our moral compass is not necessarily God's compass and we act as if it is. God will never conform to our sensibilities and has set very clear boundaries for humanity. Since the time of Adam, we have lived outside of those boundaries so much so that what should not be is now the norm. The more I study His Word, the more I truly see just how far off the mark we are and how complacent we are with being the way we are in certain areas of our lives.

We excuse premarital sex as a way of life and instead of trying to refrain from it, we often times accept the action, in confidence that God will forgive us for it. Complacent. As much as I love my friends that are openly gay and will never ostracize them, I believe their lifestyle does not line up with the word of God. Yet here recently, the trend has been what is accepted is the same as what is right.

Complacent. The Bible clearly states that we shouldn't lie, yet we tell children lies every holiday season in order to conform to the idea of Santa Clause. Better to have children believe the lie and maintain a childhood fantasy, than to tell them the true meaning of Christmas and have them be different from classmates. Complacent. Although God's thoughts are not our thoughts and His ways are not our ways, He has given us a "Blueprint" in which to know His thoughts and in which to live accordingly which is The Bible.

If you are not a part of a scripturally sound Bible study, I encourage you to join one. Although it entails a tremendous time commitment, I personally would recommend Bible Study Fellowship International. It is an intensive 7-year Bible study plan hosted in various small groups all across the world. Prior to my attending Bible College, I attended another weekly Bible study with young adults who were also thirsting for knowledge of God. Additionally, if you are a member of a church, most churches host a weekly study as well. These are examples of Bible study methods that helped set the foundation for my personal spiritual journey. However, it is crucial that you select a study that walks you through the Word from a theological, historical, and cultural standpoint so that you can have a greater understanding of His word. In addition to that group time, please spend time studying the Word for yourself. Although I have consistently attended various Bible studies, I have not always agreed with everything taught…even from my Pastor. My disagreement wasn't based on "my feelings" however, it was based on my personal study of the Word. BOTH of these are needed in order to:

1) Not believe false teachings.

2) To not rely on your own interpretation of scripture.

We live in the most technological advanced time in history and because of that, we believe we know best and can debate or disprove the Father in everything. Just as all children do with their parents as one time or another. Yet, just as children one day grow up to realize, after having fell down and gotten up, the Father really does know best.

**Reflection & Study Questions**

**1. Do you feel that God, the Father, knows best?**

**2. Have you ever encountered a false teaching of Christ and how have you responded?**

**3. Do you study the Word of God consistently via a Bible Study group or method? If not, why not?**

# Following the Leader

*"But Moses said to God, 'Who am I that I should go to Pharaoh and bring the Israelites out of Egypt?' And God said, 'I will be with you. And this will be the sign to you that it is I who have sent you: When you have brought the people out of Egypt, you will worship God on this mountain.'" Exodus 3:11-12 NIV*

*"By day the Lord went ahead of them in a pillar of cloud to guide them on their way and by night in a pillar of fire to give them light, so that they could travel by day or night. Neither the pillar of cloud by day nor the pillar of fire by night left its place in front of the people." Exodus 13:21-22 NIV*

My first opportunity to serve as a leader I failed. My freshman year in college, I was the Event Chair of a large student fashion show. In front of the crowd, the show was a success and I was high on the accolades that I received, but behind the scenes I failed and made an error. I did not realize that with leadership comes responsibility as I failed to honor an agreement with 3 of our sponsors. I may not remember the words, but I will never forget the disappointment I saw in my advisor's face after we discussed how I dropped the ball. Since then, professionally and through various commitments, I have served in a leadership capacity in some arena; as a manager of staff or a chair of a committee with 25+ people with various personalities. From that, I learned as a part of my management style to remain flexible and fluid to the suggestions of the individual's you manage, while remaining focused on your core purpose; and as a Christian, to the make sure your leadership and decisions align with the Word of God. It is not as easy as it seems. You see, leading people is the most difficult job anyone can EVER have because everyone has their own opinion of what is right and what should be done; their own belief system and moral code of right and wrong; and free will.

Although history has told the story of many great leaders, I can think of no other leader that would ever have Moses' responsibility. In the text, we find Moses leading not a few thousand people from under the rule of Pharaoh, but upwards of a million people - people who were used to living and thinking with a slave mentality. I can't begin to imagine the magnitude of the task before him. After all, God gave him the task of convincing people that a murderer was now a called man of God. He also had to show unbelievable faith in his ability to follow God and lead the Israelites to the

129

very foot of the Red Sea, as he watched the waters separate into the dry path of the future. Moses then had to encourage the Israelites to walk between two walls of water and to trust that those same waters would not come falling down upon them. But what was the key to Moses' leadership? It was not just that he himself knew how to follow, lessons he learned as he lived as a humbled shepherd, it was whom he followed, God. As we study scripture and Moses' leadership style, the one constant thing in Moses' life was that he went to the Lord with everything. With the exception of one time (which kept him from entering the promise land), in every choice, every decision, and every obstacle, he followed God's instruction. He was submissive to God.

Since that time in college, I have served as a leader and under various leaders, all of which shaped me for leadership and following, but none so much as my relationship with Christ. So I ask you, what type of leader are you? What type of follower? Each day we are called to be both, but the most important thing is not who we follow, but whom we follow, God, and what God's purpose is for our position.

**Reflection & Study Questions**

**Today you have a decision to make to choose to become a leader or a follower in certain areas of your life.**

**1. Whom and what will be your blueprint for both instances?**

**As a Christian, I believe it is always centered on the Word, not the whim of people, and will of God. Your circumstance may require you having clarity of His will, but rest assured that the biblical blueprint of His Word will never contradict that.**

# Go Tell That

*"Jesus answered and said to them, Go and tell John the things which you hear and see: The blind see and the lame walk; the lepers are cleansed and the deaf hear; the dead are raised up and the poor have the gospel preached to them. And blessed is he who is not offended because of Me." Matthew 11:4-6 NIV*

Each weekday morning, to my friends and family, I send out a good morning text with an inspirational or thought provoking scripture. It's my way of giving them some encouragement each day. One day, one of my friends specifically asked if one of my messages would turn into a devotional because they had asked themselves that same question. Why, yes and this is it.

Where is your miracle? I know that at some point in your life, if you are like me, you have asked God for a miracle. Perhaps it was a time when you wanted to see someone resurrected from the dead like Lazarus (John 11:40-43). Or a time when you wanted instantaneous healing for you or a loved one just as the woman with the issue of blood (Mark 5:25-29). Better yet, surely it was the time you needed God to multiply your finances just as Jesus made two fish and five loads feed the multitude (Matthew 14:13-21). If He can do that, then we all know that He could do anything you asked, right? I know you have waited on those very miracles at some point because I have. All of these are the miracles of Christ in the New Testament, but have you also wondered why not now? Why aren't we witnessing those same things today? Is it that Christ has lost His power – or is it that we have lost our faith?

The very first generation of disciples, even after the death and resurrection of Jesus, revolutionized the world. From a handful of believers, Christianity has become the world's largest religion with an estimated 2.2 billion followers according to a CNN report last December. Yet I must ask myself, what is our generation of disciples not doing to warrant those same miracles of the first disciples? I have a theory. In the Bible, each time we witness the miracles of Christ and those first disciples, evangelism was taking place. Each miracle was a doorway to someone learning about Christ. In this scripture, the followers of John the Baptist come to Christ because John is in prison, facing beheading, and he is wondering if Christ really is the one he had been waiting and preparing the way for (Matthew 3). In response, Christ basically replied to John's followers to tell him what they saw AND that all of these have had the gospel preached to them. That is what He has called ALL Christians to do today.

Everybody that was healed before and after the Resurrection of Christ was either actively hearing the Gospel of Christ or was an example for a Teaching of Christ. Everyone! Each miracle had a purpose and that purpose was for others to know Jesus. Jesus has not lost His power; but so many of us have lost our purpose. Go! Tell! See! If you truly want to witness a miracle, then go tell your testimony. You want unmerited grace and favor; then proclaim Him and do not be ashamed, insecure, or fearful while doing so. I am convinced that the key to living a miracle is telling the purpose of the miracle. It is not just so that someone can say, "I was cured from cancer"; it is so that someone can say "This is what Jesus did for me and let me tell you how He can do it for you". The disciples that revolutionized the world even after Christ's ascension went on to perform many miracles such as the healing of the lame (Acts 3:6-7) because they were obedient to Christ's instructions. They shared the gospel. WE are the witnesses the world needs to hear AND see. So what exactly is our witness saying about us?

In a world were nearly 2.2 billion people claim to be a Christian, I would expect to see a changed world, but we don't. We see more famine, more crime, killing, simply more (blank) than any other time in history. And although I know the Bible tells us what to expect of the end times, I think it's time WE tell our stories, don't you?

**Reflection & Study Questions**

**If this devotional has touched you in any way or convicted you, I urge you to take the first step in telling your story.**

**1. Who in your circle today needs to hear your testimony? Write a list of individuals who can benefit from your testimony.**

**2. Will you commit to seek opportunities to tell others about Christ today?**

# Encourage Yourself

*"I would have lost heart, unless I had believed that I would see the goodness of the Lord In the land of the living. Wait on the Lord; Be of good courage, And He shall strengthen your heart; Wait, I say, on the Lord!" Psalm 27:13, 14 NIV*

*"And let us not be weary in well doing, for in due season we shall reap, if we faint not. As we therefore have opportunity, let us do good unto all men, especially unto those who are of the household of faith." Galatians 6:9-10 KJV*

Well, it's been nearly five months…five months since I quit my job. Since then I have come to some startling truths about myself and have re-learned a few truths about God. The most important truth I have learned is just how much God loves me and how leaving my job, walking in obedience, has allowed me to do things I would not otherwise have done. I have been able to spend more time with my family and actually go to sleep at a decent hour since I am no longer finishing work 7 pm or later. I also am amazed with how God has blessed me with phenomenal friendships. My friends have prayed for me, fed me, sent money, and one even took me on a vacation, all without my asking or inquiring. God used them as tools for His blessings before a need ever became apparent me. Lastly, due to my leaving work, in a few days I will be going on a mission trip to the Gambia, West Africa. A mission trip I know I would not otherwise be taking if I stayed at my job, ironically, due to lack of resources and time. What does all of these blessings and God's favor have to do with today's scripture?

Although God has continually shown me grace and abundant favor during this time, it is not always easy for me to focus on the good and wait on God. It has not been easy to try and follow my dream and God's purpose for my life. It has not been easy and at times in my journey, I have grown weary in encouraging and sharing God with others while celebrating their victories, when I have wondered about my own. Yet in the midst of those moments, God gently reminds me to "not be weary of doing good" and to take heart and encourage myself. That is what I want to tell you today; how to encourage yourself.

It is easy to see the good in someone else's journey and to encourage them, but it is much harder to see the light of your own journey. However scripture gives insight into how we can encourage ourselves and remain in good spirits. We are to think upon the Lord in the "land of the living", not in this finite and earthly realm, but in the infinite Heavenly realm. When we focus on our Lord, we see a risen Savior who has already conquered life and death; therefore we should be encouraged because we know the outcome and recognize our true life begins in eternity. Secondly, we must focus on the Lord's timing and not our own. If we were to view our journey in our time, we will always come up short. But if we see our journey in incremental stages where we are waiting upon the Lord to move us, grow us, deliver us, or lead us; then we will be much more likely to view our current circumstance differently. Lastly, perhaps the greatest thing to remember in encouraging yourself is that God sees your good works and according to His time, those works will be rewarded. Our salvation is not based on our works, but God does honor the works of those who follow and honor Him. So we should not grow weary in the middle of the journey, just because we may not see progress as hoped.

So, that's what I have been learning during this season of abundant favor and doubtful moments. I have learned that by not focusing on me, but focusing on God and making Him my center, that I then am the most encouraged. I do not know what tomorrow brings for me or if the purpose of quitting my job will become manifest by my dreams coming true. Yet most of the time when I become doubtful and I wonder what am I doing with my life, I focus on Him and I know everything will be ok. And when during those times that I cannot seem to encourage myself, I reach out to my fellow believers and ask them to stand with me in prayer.

**Reflection & Study Questions**

**The next time you find yourself needing encouragement and you feel unbalanced, remember to stop focusing on you.**

**1. What can you do to stay focused on God through your trials and tribulation?**

# Where WAS He?  Questions: We Dare To Ask

*"So the sisters sent word to Jesus, "Lord, the one you love is sick." When he heard this, Jesus said, "This sickness will not end in death. No, it is for God's glory so that God's Son may be glorified through it." Now Jesus loved Martha and her sister and Lazarus. So when he heard that Lazarus was sick, he stayed where he was two more days....When Mary reached the place where Jesus was and saw him, she fell at his feet and said, "Lord, if you had been here, my brother would not have died." When Jesus saw her weeping, and the Jews who had come along with her also weeping, he was deeply moved in spirit and troubled. "Where have you laid him?" he asked. "Come and see, Lord," they replied. Jesus wept. Then the Jews said, "See how he loved him!" But some of them said, "Could not he who opened the eyes of the blind man have kept this man from dying?" Jesus, once more deeply moved, came to the tomb. It was a cave with a stone laid across the entrance. "Take away the stone," he said. "But, Lord," said Martha, the sister of the dead man, "by this time there is a bad odor, for he has been there four days." Then Jesus said, "Did I not tell you that if you believe, you will see the glory of God?" John 11:3-6, 32-40 NIV*

Can you imagine Mary and Martha's frustration?  They had served Jesus, had Him in their home, but the moment they needed Him most, He didn't come. The Lord made the deliberate choice to delay in coming to Lazarus.  Why?

Last week, my friend asked me to address why God would allow the tragedy of Aurora or Sandy Hook or any other tragedy to happen and I admit I initially wanted to refuse to address it.  I am not a theologian nor an ordained minister (yet ☺) so I felt that it was not my place to address it.  But then, God spoke to me.  Why not me?  These devotionals are not just written to teach others, but to share my walk as a Christian so that other believers won't think they suffer, stumble, or in this case question alone.  I did not question Aurora, but I have questioned tragedy and suffering before...from my aunt who was killed by a drunk driver to the uncle I never met because he was shot and killed before I was born.  I have witnessed the days and years after violence and tragedy occurred in my own family and have asked God, "why?"

What is the purpose of pain?  Why would the God I love and serve allow such a tragedy?  What sense is there to be made from any of it?

135

The same sense that Jesus' delay in visiting Lazarus made. Every miracle in the Bible was for God's glory. Every miracle. So even in Jesus allowing Lazarus to die, God would receive glory by Lazarus' resurrection. But more importantly others would come to witness and know the saving grace of Christ. This delay pointed to Christ's own resurrection and salvation. But even so, doesn't it seem selfish of God? Doesn't it seem like God is playing with our lives so He can receive glory? To an unbeliever yes it would and this is where many believers and unbelievers stumble.

Each person that was killed in tragedy was loved more by God than by their families. God loves everyone you love more than you do or even can. We are His children. Tragedies serve a threefold purpose; it has brings Christians together and allows reconciliation for many to come back to God. Tragedy often times brings people closer to a true relationship with God. Just as most children run to their parents bed when the "boogie monster" comes out at night, so do God's errant children (us) run to His waiting arms – as we should. The tragedy has allowed God to receive the glory even in the midst of that great evil. How so? Prayers have gone up, people are standing in expectation of God doing the miraculous and He already has done so. Days after the tragedy in Aurora a baby was born who mother survived unscathed, but whose father is in a medically induced coma recovering from near fatal injuries. Even as evil things are done, blessings and miracles still circumvent what others meant for evil. Evil never wins and the minutes and days of the aftermath prove that simply by the resiliency of the human spirit. God's glory is in our spirit as we were made in His image. But lastly, those we have lost are now home. We become so tied to this life that we falsely believe this is all there is and it isn't. The life we are living, the successes we have, are but a poor imitation of what true and abundant life with God looks like. Those that know Him have crossed over into the eternal victory and they have returned to a place of joy and peace. For all of our pious prayers, no matter the manner that a person dies, for believers, to die is to gain (Philippians 1:21). So although we are left with the tragedy and heartbreak of living without them, they have been restored to their original form and purpose. There is no tragedy in that.

I cannot answer why tragedy and suffering occurs. I cannot fathom the work of God's hand, but I can fathom His heart as I have seen it directed towards me many times before. When I have questioned God with those very same questions, this is what He has revealed and told me; there is a purpose and plan for everything. We often ask where God was when "x" happens, but rest assured that He was right there in the midst of it all.

**Reflection & Study Questions**

**1. Do you struggle with believing in God in the face or horrific events and crimes? You are not alone. Write down the questions that you have for God and pray for His revelation.**

**2. Explain what it means for God to be sovereign? Do you believe God is sovereign?**

**3. Do you feel Christians have the right to question God? Why or Why not?**

Shaniqua Rischer

## Lord, I Believe, But…

*"So they brought him. When the spirit saw Jesus, it immediately threw the boy into a convulsion. He fell to the ground and rolled around, foaming at the mouth. Jesus asked the boy's father, "How long has he been like this?" "From childhood," he answered. "It has often thrown him into fire or water to kill him. But if you can do anything, take pity on us and help us." "If you can?" said Jesus. "Everything is possible for one who believes." Immediately the boy's father exclaimed, "I do believe; help me overcome my unbelief!" Mark 9: 20-24 NIV*

*"Then the disciples came to Jesus in private and asked, "Why couldn't we drive it out?" He replied, "Because you have so little faith. Truly I tell you, if you have faith as small as a mustard seed, you can say to this mountain, "Move from here to there and it will move. Nothing will be impossible for you." Matthew 17:19-20 NIV*

The Bible is full of inspiring scripture. Scripture that speaks to your Spirit, convicts you, and heals you. However as I write this, I am hard press to think of a scripture that is more "real" than this one in Mark 9. For many Christians, the issue is not in our believing it is in our unbelief.

This father stood before Jesus and admitted what we all, at times shamefully, struggle with - our unbelief. How can we encourage others and not believe? How can we witness what He did yesterday yet still doubt today? Yet we do. Yet I do. More honestly, how can we have faith in the unknown and unimaginable, when all we've ever seen and known is the opposite? When Jesus inquired to the father about his son, Christ knew that this man had witnessed his son struggle for years. He knew this father struggled to have hope (the foundation for faith) when He spoke to him.

As for the father, can you imagine his desperation? How many "healers" had he gone to before? How many things had he tried by his own hand? He even brought the boy to Christ's disciples yet they could not heal his son. He had experienced disappointment after disappointment; let down after let down. This was truly all he had ever known; all he ever saw his son to be. And then he encounters Jesus and he dares to think, he dares to say "if you can..."

I can relate more so to the father than I would care to admit and I beat myself up because of it. I tell myself that I must always exhibit faith, but then I think upon this scripture and I recognize if I cannot admit my unbelief to God who can I admit it to? The father in this scripture was not afraid to admit his shortcomings to Jesus and show his doubt, while at the same time asking Jesus to intercede on his son's behalf. He did. Because of that mustard seed size faith, Jesus healed his son and caste out demons. Jesus took a little faith and turned it into the imaginable and now real. Where the man once doubted, he now believed because he saw the fruition of his seed of belief. And I am learning that's all that Jesus requires from us sometimes. Yes He wants us to always operate in great faith, but our Lord also knows those times that we can't. He is aware of those situations that all we have to give is the smallest seed of faith and thankfully, that's all He needs. Those seeds can turn into a harvest you never thought to reap, feeding us for future times of doubts and droughts. Jesus has always shown Himself to make bountiful out of a little. So where do you only have a seed of faith?

Today, in one area of my life, all I have is a kernel...a small seed... of belief to give Jesus. Last week a friend told me he doesn't even think I believe God to show up in this area and I must admit that by my past words, he is right. I haven't spoken as if I believe. But I also know that I have hope and I have the best kernel of faith I can give right now. Everything I have is wrapped up in that kernel- my hopes and dreams-just as that father long ago had hopes and dreams for his child. What about you? Is there a situation facing you were all you can muster is a seed of faith? As I stand before Him, my Savior, I am saying "Lord, I believe. Help my unbelief." And I do...and He shall.


### Reflection & Study Questions

**1. Do you have a situation where you are struggling to believe and give your seed to Christ?**

**2. What has Christ revealed to you about the situation?**

Shaniqua Rischer

## I Think I'm Better Than You...

*"All of us have become like one who is unclean, and all our righteous acts are like filthy rags; we all shrivel up like a leaf, and like the wind our sins sweep us away." Isaiah 64:6 NIV*

*"For all have sinned and fall short of the glory of God..." Romans 3:23 NIV*

*"When they kept on questioning Him [Jesus], He straightened up and said to them, "Let any one of you who is without sin be the first to throw a stone at her." John 8:7 NIV*

I think I'm better than you...I think I clean up more than you...I think I work harder than you...I think I am holier than you...I think I am. How many of us can honestly say that we think that about ourselves in some context? Be it in our marriages, family, and place of employment or otherwise? It's the dirty little truth that no one wants to admit. And in some instances, it's true. Someone is cleaner than I am, someone may worker harder than I do and I can guarantee you someone is faster than me (Usain Bolt proved he is faster than all of us). We can freely admit those things, but what about when I behave and think that I am better than you? Holier than you? Better yet, what if you believe it about me?

In 2012, gay-marriage debates and a Chick-Fil-A "buy-in" occurred where believers and non-believers alike weighed in on what's right and what's wrong. I have too. Yet while were having these discussions and events, I am concerned about what are lasting effects we may cause one another.

We are losing our compassion for others because we do not understand the compassion that has been shown towards us. Instead, in subtle and not so subtle ways, we are becoming judgmental, critical, and legalistic with our faith - the very things that Jesus came to tear down and destroy. We say that all sin is equal, but do we really treat others like that?

I have come to the conclusion that many of us struggle with the "better than" syndrome. Myself included. What is the "better than" syndrome? Simply put, it's when you think you are better than you are. It's an easy trap to fall into. Just because I don't struggle with sex or drugs, I think I am better than the person that does. Just because someone is healthier and lives a fit lifestyle, they are better than the obese and sedentary person. Or because I haven't raped, maimed, or killed someone then surely I am better than all those who have. Surely at least them. Yet how does God see us? When the adulterous woman was brought before Christ by her accusers, instead of condemnation, Christ said "let he who is without sin caste the first stone". No one did. However today, we seem to have forgotten this because in every aspect of our lives I am seeing people caste stones. They are casting them in politics, in the church, in their homes, in our schools, or on Face Book and Twitter. If it saddens me, how much more is our Father saddened?

I am overweight and by medical standards; I am actually obese – even if it is stretched out over six feet. But it wasn't until this week that I finally asked God for forgiveness for my sin of obesity. I never saw this as my sin. What sin you may ask? For letting food become my crutch and seeking it for comfort instead of seeking God; for living to eat and allowing food to become a stronghold of the flesh instead of eating to live; and more than anything, for all the times I treated my body more like a landfill than a temple (1 Corinthians 6:19-20).

I use the example of my food and weight struggle because realistically I am no better than my friends that struggle with sex or those that struggle with lying, etc. No matter how I front. Most think like me and would never have seen the sin in that, but there is. I am no better than the person that drinks in excess or uses drugs. Our sins are manifested differently, but they are still sins, in public or private.

We all have our opinions of right and wrong, however God and His word are the supreme authority and our standards fall short of His. No one is without sin and we are all imperfect people and as Christians, we should remember that before casting stones. I believe that there are many things that are acceptable in our cultures which are in direct contradiction to His word, but I also stand by His grace and mercy. Without it, I would not be covered and neither would you.

I do not believe in tolerance for sin and will always speak the truth of His word in love (I am not the sugar-coating kind either), but other than the scriptures that point to Christ as my Savior and the importance of loving the Lord, the scripture we should most honor is loving our neighbors just as well as we love ourselves (Matthew 22:39). In a world that places importance on the hierarchy, successes, and failures of others we should all remember that.

141

We all struggle. We are all imperfect.

This week, before you speak against someone or have thoughts of judgment, remember that we are all equal. Our best falls short of the mark of eternity and if not for the grace, mercy, and love of the Lord, where would you be?

**Reflection & Study Questions**

**1. Do you agree with that obesity can be looked at as a sin?**

**2. What other areas in our lives have become sinful yet we do not recognize it? Write them down.**

**2. Do you believe that God can deliver you from that sinful condition? What can you do to help your own deliverance?**

## Something in the Water

*"But blessed are those who trust in the Lord and have made the Lord their hope and confidence. They are like trees planted along a riverbank, with roots that reach deep into the water. Such trees are not bothered by the heat or worried by long months of drought. Their leaves stay green, and they never stop producing fruit." Jeremiah 17:7-8 NLT*

*"Jesus replied, "If you only knew the gift God has for you and who you are speaking to, you would ask me, and I would give you living water." John 4:10 NLT*

At the beginning of August, I had six very good friends that were pregnant. Since then, one has delivered a beautiful baby girl and as I type this, one is in labor to deliver her first child. If everything goes as expected, God willing, two more will deliver their children before August concludes. I know, what you are thinking, there MUST be something in the water here! I agree... Yet what do all of these women have in common besides the obvious...that Winter 2011 was fruitful?!? LOL. Hope. They each have hope. Each of these women has carried their blessing for months and has prayed daily in anticipation of holding their child in their hands. They all hope to see each labor pain, every sleepless night, the discomfort of pregnancy result in the birth of a healthy child. What have you been hoping for?

Although you may not be expecting a child right now, you are in the process of birthing a future dream, praying over a situation, and waiting to see the fruit of your labor. All of that equates to you having hope. You hope your dream will come true, your prayers will be answered, and that the wait will be worth it. You hope. We all hope. And you know what? It's hard to hope because sometimes you wonder when will hope turn into the actual. And for some, they try not to hope because they don't want to be disappointed. I know I have been guilty of that more than once. Have you?

Yet, when I read these two scriptures, I was struck by how hope and trust in the Lord are described as a parallel to deep waters that nourish those that draw from them. And what better deep waters to be nourished by than the living water of Christ? When Christ spoke to the woman at the well, He said something I never noticed before; "If you only knew the gift God has for you ..." Hope is directly tied to what our Father wants to give us. Hope is the knowledge that our Father, God, has something better for us. We know

143

it even if we don't see it. We believe that God has a gift for us simply because of who we are to Him - His beloved children.

Each time I try not to hope, hope comes back. It rears its beautiful head in my Spirit and I start to hope again. I can't help it and I am starting to realize that hope is just as important as whatever I am hoping for. Hope teaches us to rely on God and stand in expectation of answered prayers. Hope teaches us to draw deep in ourselves to do what we didn't think we could do. Hope prepares us for the moment that dreams come to fruition. Hope teaches us how to wait and perhaps, most important of all, hope allows us to live in those "in the meantime" moments. You see for believers, hope does not originate with us. Instead, hope springs forth from living waters so it's no wonder that hope is a part of the very fabric of our faith and walk with Christ.

Although I joked about their being something in the water for me to be surrounded by so many pregnant women at once, I recognize the truth of that for all believers. There is something in the water that allows us to hope and keep going, keep seeking, and keep waiting to receive God's best for us. No matter your dream, today, I want to encourage you to keep hoping. If only you knew the blessing that is to come from that hope, you would understand why it is so important to do just that.

**Reflection & Study Questions**

**1. Do you find yourself becoming discouraged because you haven't seen your hopes and dreams come true? What have you learned in the delay?**

**2. In what area of your life do you need to keep hoping today?**

## Sacrifice and Obedience: The Experiment Update

*"Then Paul said: 'I am a Jew, born in Tarsus of Cilicia, but brought up in this city. I studied under Gamaliel and was thoroughly trained in the law of our ancestors. I was just as zealous for God as any of you are today. I persecuted the followers of this Way to their death, arresting both men and women and throwing them into prison, as the high priest and all the Council can themselves testify. I even obtained letters from them to their associates in Damascus, and went there to bring these people as prisoners to Jerusalem to be punished. About noon as I came near Damascus, suddenly a bright light from heaven flashed around me. I fell to the ground and heard a voice say to me, 'Saul! Saul! Why do you persecute me?' "'Who are you, Lord?' I asked. "'I am Jesus of Nazareth, whom you are persecuting,' he replied…"'What shall I do, Lord?' I asked. "'Get up,' the Lord said, 'and go into Damascus. There you will be told all that you have been assigned to do.' Acts 22: 3-10 NIV*

*"There he [Paul] met a Jew named Aquila, a native of Pontus, who had recently come from Italy with his wife Priscilla, because Claudius had ordered all Jews to leave Rome. Paul went to see them, and because he was a tentmaker as they were, he stayed and worked with them." Acts 18: 2-3 NIV*

I have a serious question to ask you. How much are you willing to sacrifice for Christ in order to be obedient to God? Before you read any further, I want you to pause and think. Now, for some, sacrifice means giving financially and for others sacrifice may equate to giving time. Many parents work two jobs, sacrifice sleep and relationships so their kids can have access to the best schools, newer clothes, or even the latest gadget, toy, or cell phone and that's just for their kids. Yet my question for you and for each of us, "How much are you (we) willing to sacrifice for Christ in order to be obedient?" I am finding out the answer myself in new ways every day. I just spent nearly a thousand dollars on a vision for the ministry I believe God has revealed to me. As a person that has no job, but a mortgage, that should tell you just how important this vision and ministry is to me.

Most people whose professions are in ministry are not wealthy. This doesn't mean that God has called His servants to be paupers, but it doesn't mean He has called them to have riches either; it simply means He is using them in different ways to teach and preach the gospel. When I had my calling experience to preach years ago (which took me nearly a decade to call it what it was), a part of that was my belief that I would be known on a worldwide stage. Whether that comes to pass or not, remains to be seen, but I associated riches and fame with it. You got it, I saw myself "Big Willie" style! Yet as I wrote that check, it dawned on me that the survival and thriving of the ministry has become more important than the survival of me. And this is where our text takes us.

Paul was a learned, highly educated, Roman citizen but instead of using his learning to gain wealth or prestige, Paul lived humbly. He worked as a tent maker and depended on the kindness of the church to support him when necessary. Instead of using his education, Paul chose instead to travel as a missionary to teach, preach, and disciple others in their walk as Christians. Paul loved Christ so much he literally sacrificed his life to obey and follow the Lord's instructions.

Years ago I promised God to follow Him; do whatever He called me to do; go wherever He called me to go. Naively, I never would have imagined exactly what living for Christ would entail and some of the sacrifices I have had to make as I tried to be obedient. I wonder if Paul felt and thought the same way.

Unlike someone who was laid off, the decision to leave my job was my own and where I felt my obedience to God was leading me. Recently, my sister hired me to clean an abandoned home for $250. Having bills to pay and needing the money, I quickly jumped at the chance to work. Yet it dawned on me that I wasn't earning money to purchase my new favorite pair of shoes from Nordstrom, to buy my next pair of $200 jeans or even to go on my next great vacation. I was cleaning because of sacrifice and obedience. I am dedicated to getting this ministry off the ground and living the life I believe Christ has called me to live (hopefully He calls me to a Saks 5th Avenue and Neiman Marcus experience next, LOL). Those things are no longer my priority; instead every dime I make now is in the context of how can this go to bless and grow the ministry God has given me, as well as support my basic needs. As my mindset changes, I am learning what it really means to sacrifice and be obedient. I am beginning to understand why and how Paul gave it all up to follow the will of Christ. Paul's (previously Saul) experience with Christ on the road to Damascus changed him so much that sacrifice no longer was sacrifice. It then became his lifestyle of obedience.

So my question to you is what are you willing to sacrifice in order to obey? What sacrifice are you making in order to be obedient and follow where God is leading you? And by follow, it may not be the call to ministry in the conventional sense. We each have different roles in the body of Christ, but as Christians He is calling you to something i.e. teaching, coaching little league, adopting a child, writing a book, becoming a Christian actor/screenwriter in Hollywood, cooking in a soup kitchen, or owning a business built on Christian principles to help fellow Christians live a better life. There is something for you to do, but you must answer the call and accept the call. Whatever He is calling you to do will require a sacrifice explicitly from you in obedience to Him.

My fellow brothers and sisters in Christ, I am trying to walk in obedience and I will not lie, it has required sacrifice of parts of my life that I want. Sometimes I have doubts and my obedience has gone against not only the logic of others, but my own too. But obedience is becoming a lifestyle for me, evident to those who know me. The sacrifice of self and obedience to Him has brought a peace that surpasses all understanding (Philippians 4:7). Through sacrifice and obedience you learn to give all worry to Him; you pray differently; you think differently; and you love differently, all because your sacrifice becomes your obedience and your obedience becomes a lifestyle. This is what a true relationship with Christ requires. Before Damascus, the world would have never known an educated man by the name of Saul. After Damascus the man once called Saul, now Paul, became a humble tent maker whose sacrifice and obedience has mentored many throughout the ages, myself include.

My prayer to those that read this is for you to take the first step of obedience to Christ, and sacrifice your "self" to Him as you follow Him wherever He leads. I haven't missed a meal nor missed a bill since I started walking this journey of obedience.

**Reflection & Study Questions**

**1. What sacrifice are you making in order to be obedient and follow where God is leading you?**

**2. What has this sacrifice cost you?**

Shaniqua Rischer

## Martha, When Will We Learn…?

*"As Jesus and his disciples were on their way, he came to a village where a woman named Martha opened her home to him. 39 She had a sister called Mary, who sat at the Lord's feet listening to what he said. 40 But Martha was distracted by all the preparations that had to be made. She came to him and asked, "Lord, don't you care that my sister has left me to do the work by myself? Tell her to help me!" "Martha, Martha," the Lord answered, "you are worried and upset about many things, but few things are needed—or indeed only one. Mary has chosen what is better, and it will not be taken away from her."* Luke 10: 38-42 NIV

I over slept again. I had a long night of replying to e-mails, doing work that I didn't get a chance to do during the day because I was working for my sister, and having a conference call with my Minister's in Training Group. I wake up and immediately think about the scripture text for the day I need to send to my friends and family; since I overslept. I am late and yep there it is! The ding of a text message from a friend asking if everything is o.k. with me since I haven't sent today's text. I find the text, send it out and immediately rush to get dressed to go work with my sister again, all the while taking breaks to respond to e-mails that are coming in from people asking for my feedback on whichever project I have committed myself. I write reminders for myself for the devotional I need to write, the agenda for the ministry meeting I will be having soon, and preparing notes for the mission trip that my church will be embarking upon in 2013. In the day of my life…what did I forget?

*"Martha, Martha" the Lord answered…*

No matter how hard I try, no matter how many reminders I set or the promise I make to God, I simply struggle with being Martha. I get so caught up in doing all the things/tasks of my life, including ministry, that I simply forget to spend time with Him for myself.

*"You are worried and upset about many things, but few things are needed—or indeed only one."*

When I first read this biblical account (and several times after), I agreed with Martha. Mary needed to get up and work. Just like Martha, I would have been quick to point it out. Yet Mary had it right all along. You can do nothing without first being in the presence of the Master. Even Jesus recognized the need to do this. Throughout the New Testament we are given accounts of Christ rising early to spend time with the Father or separating Himself to be in counsel and conversation with God.

As much as I love the Lord and try to dedicate my mornings to Him or even times throughout the day, ***unless I am diligent about it***, I find myself focusing on everything that I need to do or take care of versus spending the most important moments with Him. Yet just as Christ pointed out to Martha and continually points out to me, the most important time spent during my day is the time I spend with Him. Everything else is second fiddle, including doing ministry. Christ understood that when we don't slow down to be in His presence, our days become fruitless instead of fruitful.

*"Mary has chosen what is better, and it will not be taken away from her."*

It is a daily struggle for me and I do mean daily to turn myself from Martha into Mary, but I am being made over into a new creature in more ways than one. Guess what? I am not the one doing it. The Spirit is. How many of you struggle with that just as I do? I suspect more do than do not in our always "on", always accessible, always catching up society.

Yet in order to have a relationship with Him, it takes concentrated effort on our parts to sit still and simply be at His feet and listen to Him as He engages us in conversation. This week, on one of my FB acquaintances pages, someone posted about their being at the gym at 5 am. However, the ironic thing is that he also posts about being at the gym at 9 pm, at 5 pm, on Saturdays and Sundays. He is passionate about bodybuilding and it is reflected in his physique. As I read that post last week, it dawned on me just why I struggle so much with losing weight again. You see, I am not that dedicated to it. I once was. The same can be said about our spiritual lives and our relationships with Christ. The prayers and the bible study that you did last week or even last year, will not get you through today. A relationship with Christ takes time spent daily, a daily dose of "I love you", and a committed and diligent effort to nourish that relationship-daily. The work we put into our relationship with Him will then be reflected in our emotional and spiritual physique.

So although I am Martha (which definitely has a time and place), I am becoming Mary as well (which is necessary every day). My relationship with Christ requires it. Doesn't yours?

**Reflection & Study Questions**

**1. Which are you: Martha or Mary?**

**2. What were the characteristics of both Martha and Mary? List the good and bad.**

**3. Where in your life is God calling you to be both?**

# I've Been Changed

*"Then he asked them, 'But who do you say I am?' Simon Peter answered, 'You are the Messiah, the Son of the living God.' Jesus replied, 'You are blessed, Simon son of John, because my Father in heaven has revealed this to you. You did not learn this from any human being. Now I say to you that you are Peter (which means 'rock'), and upon this rock I will build my church, and all the powers of hell will not conquer it. And I will give you the keys of the Kingdom of Heaven. Whatever you forbid on earth will be forbidden in heaven, and whatever you permit on earth will be permitted in heaven.'" Matthew 16:15-18 NIV*

"I've been changed: healed, freed, delivered. I've found: joy, peace, grace and favor…"

These are the opening lyrics of one of my favorite gospel songs by William McDowell, I Won't Go Back.  The song resonates with me because it is the testimony of "before and after"; the "before and after" moments of accepting Christ AND developing a relationship with Christ. The beauty of the "before and after" is that initially, to the naked eye…the non-spiritual eye…, the "before and after" is undetectable. However, undetectable to others initially, there is still a "before and after" moment for those that know Christ. This morning, my Pastor made a comment that served as affirmation for a lot of my conversations this year. Without quoting him exactly, he reiterated from a biblical perspective, when God changed someone's name to indicate a new direction or promise for their life (i.e. Abram to Abraham in Genesis 17:5 and Jacob to Israel in Genesis 32:28) that name change often happened privately before it took place publically.  Here in the text, Jesus announces to Simon (who is now to be Peter) his future anointing for his life, seemingly before he was prepared to walk in that anointing.

Although I haven't been given a new name, I have been given a new vision and purpose.  Well, it was new to me. When I think back I recall my own journey and relationship with Christ and just how much I have changed. Recently, I posted the following on my personal Face Book page:

*"I remember 11 years ago when I was asked to pray out loud at bible study, I looked at the person CRAZY and said "no"… I remember about 7 years ago, when I cussed a friend out RIGHT before we were to pray over the meal cause he wouldn't stop talking and we were*

*waiting on him before we could bless the food... And tonight, as the leader of our women's mission team to Ghana asked me to close us out in prayer; I had a 2-second pause before agreeing and praying thinking "I don't know about you, but I KNOW I'VE BEEN CHANGED!!!"*

If you would have told me 11 years ago that I would not only feel comfortable praying out loud, but was to become a minister and preach a sermon, I would have called you crazy. As much as I claimed to love God back then, I simply would not have accepted that for my life. Yet, God in His infinite wisdom has spent many days and nights speaking to me about the change being manifested in my life. And guess what? Not everyone wants to see me change. Not because they wish me ill will, but because they are simply use to the old me and desire to maintain that same type of relationship with me. Do you know when God changes you, ultimately you cannot go back to the person you used to be? There is no peace in that life. You may be drawn to parts of it, but there is no peace. Something is missing.

Additionally with one of my close friends, I felt the need to explain the change in me until one day I recognized it simply wasn't their concern. What God has spoken to me about my life is the vision He has for MY life. That doesn't include getting others on board. It simply means I am to stay true to what He has spoken in order to produce fruit.

Have any of you felt that way? You know God has spoken something to you, spoken the vision of a new you, but others won't let you grow into that vision? Or perhaps others encourage you to grow, but you yourself are grasping to hold onto the old you? Or perhaps you are like Peter? Christ has spoken the vision for your life and although you act as if you understand, you haven't experienced the other side of the cross to even know exactly what has been spoken to you? I understand.

I am here to tell you that it's ok to change. Yes, I know you think you know that. But if you truly know it, then why are you fighting Him so much? Why are you fighting the pruning process? Why are you struggling to hold onto the life you know so well because you can't imagine the life He wants to give you? You can't imagine anything different. It's all you know. See, I told you I understand. Today, know that it is ok to change. It's ok to let go of you. I'm on the other side of the cross – the "before and after" and I can testify that it's ok. Is it always easy? No. Will there be trials and tribulations in my future? Yes. Am I in for the fight of my life with the enemy? Yes. But the Bible tells us that every person that God changed through relationship stayed changed and pressed forward towards the vision He gave them. If you don't believe me, just ask Peter. He gives a way better testimony than I could ever give.

### Reflection & Study Questions

**1. Why are you struggling to hold onto the life you know so well because you can't imagine the life He wants to give you?**

**Exercise:**

**Take a piece of paper and make 2 columns: the "Haves" and the "Have Not". List your struggles under "Haves". Now, if you were to let go of those things that you struggle under the "Haves" with, what could you possibly gain? List the things you could gain under the "Have Not" column. Are the struggles worth it?**

Shaniqua Rischer

## My Life Is My Worship

*"I desire to do your will, my God; your law is within my heart." Psalm 40:8 NIV*

*"For physical training is of some value, but godliness has value for all things, holding promise for both the present life and the life to come. This is a trustworthy saying that deserves full acceptance. 10 That is why we labor and strive, because we have put our hope in the living God, who is the Savior of all people, and especially of those who believe. Command and teach these things. Don't let anyone look down on you because you are young, but set an example for the believers in speech, in conduct, in love, in faith and in purity. Until I come, devote yourself to the public reading of Scripture, to preaching and to teaching. Do not neglect your gift, which was given you through prophecy when the body of elders laid their hands on you. Be diligent in these matters; give yourself wholly to them, so that everyone may see your progress. Watch your life and doctrine closely. Persevere in them, because if you do, you will save both yourself and your hearers." 1 Timothy 4:8-16 NIV*

My life is my worship. At least I try to make it my worship. I sincerely try to live a life that is reflecting of my worship and glory to the Lord. Just as with anything, some days I do well, but some days I do not. Every once in a while I get in one of my disobedient moods, meaning I do something I really have no business doing. It doesn't come often, but when it does and I give in to my disobedience, usually the consequence happens fairly quickly for me. Or, God will block the wrong that I was planning from taking place. It used to frustrate me until I realized that was God's way of protecting me. Grace is not to be dismissed or devalued. Also, I don't know about you all, but whenever I do or say ANYTHING not of God now, the Holy Spirit convicts me with quickness. Within the day, I am either apologizing to someone and feel the need to make amends (even if they are not ready to receive it). Yet how do you make amends to God for willful disobedience? You don't. Instead you ask for forgiveness and mercy living a life that is pleasing to Him.

Right now, I feel like being willfully disobedient to God. I feel like doing me. Yet I realize that someone is watching my worship, someone is watching my walk and that is more important to me than the momentary satisfaction of disobedience. Why? Because just as Paul wrote this letter to Timothy to encourage him in his walk with Christ, I realize that in the age we live in many people are seeking healing, seeking truth, seeking deliverance, seeking a new life, and are seeking God. I am saddened because honestly, not many are finding what they are seeking. Although I have been called to serve God in a very distinct way, so has each person that is a Christian. People are looking at our walk and wondering what sets us apart from those that don't believe in Christ? I look and wonder the same thing.

I have served as a Big before (Big Brothers Big Sisters) and one of the most important things you learn as a mentor is to not only be present with your mentee, but to set an example. That can be said in all areas of our life. Athletes have examples of those gone before them in the sport who achieved their goals, business executives have coaches that serve as mentors in their professional careers, and even pastors and preachers have "fathers or mothers" in the ministry. What about the rest of us? Who serves as our example? The godly and right answer should be Christ, but the more conversations I have with others, I recognize that many are getting Christ second hand. They hear pieces of scriptures out of context and try to piece together a relationship with Christ. They are not studying His word for themselves, in the context of a good bible study under a Christ-centered leader. Many are learning by watching you. Yes, YOU.

I recognize we are all on an evolutionary journey in Christ, but at some point, we must die to ourselves to fully live for Him. When we do that, we then become the example of Christ that teaches others. We save not only ourselves, but our hearers and seers as well.

This week I challenge each of you to be more aware of the example of faith and belief in Christ you set through your words, actions, and deeds. Do your children know about Christ not only because of what you teach them, but because of how you live? Does your boss and co-workers know you are a Christian, not because of the gospel and Christian music you listen to during work, but instead because of how you show restraint, integrity, and excellence in your work? Do strangers know you are a Christian not because of the fish symbol on your car, but because of how you stop to help the homeless, widows, children and disenfranchised of our society? It is one thing to say what you are and another thing to live what you are.

Shaniqua Rischer

**Reflection & Study Questions**

**1. So my question is what type of example are you setting?**

**2. Does your name of Christian match the walk of Christian?**

# No Record

*"LORD, if you kept a record of our sins, who, O Lord, could ever survive? But you offer forgiveness, that we might learn to fear you. I am counting on the LORD; yes, I am counting on him. I have put my hope in his word. I long for the Lord more than sentries long for the dawn....O Israel, hope in the LORD; for with the LORD there is unfailing love. His redemption overflows." Psalm 130:3-7 NLT*

Have you ever realized just how much you've been forgiven? Just how much God loves you? Do you really know? If you know how much you've been forgiven, then why do so many of us struggle with forgiving others and ourselves?

During service my Pastor made a statement that stayed with me, "When God forgives He is done with it". When I heard the statement, it gave me comfort because there are things I want no record of, especially with God. What about when people forgive? Are we ever done with it? I realized a lot people – I included – struggle with forgiveness and keeping no record because we simply cannot imagine being "done with it". Instead, we revisit the scene of the memory over and over again, even after we have asked for forgiveness of our own actions or have tried to forgive others. We make mistakes and make wrong choices. We all have experienced hurt and betrayal at the hands of others. Yet instead of choosing to heal, we spend so much time and energy beating ourselves up and holding on to bitterness, never fully letting go and forgiving.

And that is where the devil would lead us to believe we should stay, in bitterness and regret. He loves when we don't forgive ourselves or others because that is the doorway to a stronghold on our hearts and spirits. Unforgiveness becomes the entryway for bitterness, defeat, and stagnation.

Yet that is not how God would choose us to live. He wants us to have life, a redeemed life.

If you want to learn how to forgive others, you must first learn how to forgive yourself. If you want to learn how to forgive yourself, you must first understand just how much you have been forgiven and the love behind that forgiveness. Nothing we have done, big or small, can separate us from the love of God (Romans 8:35). Not even ourselves. One thing that God revealed to me about those who had hurt me was my role in the hurt. Now, this doesn't apply in all situations because there are situations with children/adults or of violence, etc. where the victim had no part in the injustice. However, the people and situations that hurt me the most are situations that I ignored the warning signs or prolonged a situation beyond what I knew I should. In other words I was not blameless. Therefore, in my bitterness towards them, I had to recognize my own hand in the situation. I had to accept and forgive myself then I understood what "being done with it" meant and I was able to forgive.

The devil seeks to keep us in bondage and repeating memories or situations because we refuse to forgive. However, it is those very things we hold on that God has already forgiven us. He has no record of it. The greatest wrong would be choosing to stay in bondage to a choice or memory from which God has already freed us.

God loves each of us so much, that even when we hurt Him through our sin and disobedience, He invites us to come before Him and experience true forgiveness. A forgiveness that is not conditional on anything that we can do, but what His son Jesus Christ has already done. That's how much God loves us. How much He loves you.

Until we truly understand what it means to be done with it and to forgive, we will continue to live a life that is an imitation of the one God has intended for us.

## Reflection & Study Questions

**Think about the list of "Haves and Haves not".**

**1. What things could you have if you let them go?**

**2. What areas or people do you need to forgive? By you not forgiving, does this help or hinder you?**

**3. How can you gain peace for yourself and heal? Even if the person is no longer in your presence (out of state, country or deceased).**

# Besides Every Man: His Choice

*"If you keep quiet at a time like this, deliverance and relief for the Jews will arise from some other place, but you and your relatives will die. Who knows if perhaps you were made queen for just such a time as this?" Esther 4:14 NLT "So the king and Haman went to Queen Esther's banquet, and as they were drinking wine on the second day, the king again asked, "Queen Esther, what is your petition? It will be given you. What is your request? Even up to half the kingdom, it will be granted." Then Queen Esther answered, "If I have found favor with you, Your Majesty, and if it pleases you, grant me my life—this is my petition. And spare my people—this is my request." Esther 7:1-3 NLT*

*"Jezebel his wife said, "Is this how you act as king over Israel? Get up and eat! Cheer up. I'll get you the vineyard of Naboth the Jezreelite."So she wrote letters in Ahab's name, placed his seal on them, and sent them to the elders and nobles who lived in Naboth's city with him. In those letters she wrote: "Proclaim a day of fasting and seat Naboth in a prominent place among the people. But seat two scoundrels opposite him and have them bring charges that he has cursed both God and the king. Then take him out and stone him to death."… "There was never anyone like Ahab, who sold himself to do evil in the eyes of the Lord, urged on by Jezebel his wife. He behaved in the vilest manner by going after idols, like the Amorites the Lord drove out before Israel." 1 Kings 21:7-10, 25-26 NIV*

This week, on various media outlets and social media sites, I saw a beautiful picture of First Lady Michelle Obama hugging her husband, President Barak Obama, from behind with a thrilled smile on her face. There has been a lot of talk about the First Lady, some good and some bad, but that picture made me think about the importance of a woman in a man's life. It also made me think about the legacies of two Queens.

The first Queen was Esther; a young woman of Jewish decent that became the wife of the Persian King Xerxes. The book of Esther reads like a novel of political intrigue, but more than anything it is about how one woman recognized that her life and everything decision before was in preparation for a specific time. Her sacrifice was necessary for the survival of her people, her family, and ensured that her husband did not commit a grievous injustice against God's anointed people, the Jews. Her life and sacrifice is still remembered and honored today.

159

The second Queen is just as memorable. She too has been immortalized throughout history. Her name was Jezbel. She plotted not just for financial gain, she plotted for recognition and power amongst all at the expense of God's anointed. Alongside her husband, she ruled with trickery and manipulation, was murderous and worshipped false idols.

Both women and their husbands fascinate me. You see, rather it be a Jezebel or an Esther, I recognize that in the end, men truly choose who their mate will be. A man can choose the woman that will support and uplift him, as well as guide and advise them in Godly decisions. Or a man can choose a woman that is manipulating, divisive, and disdains the Word of God. The influence of a woman is powerful in a man's life and whichever type they choose; it is a reflection of them. So gentleman, who is reflecting you and how are you being reflected?

However, as a woman, I also recognize that I too have a choice. I decide the type of woman and mate I will be. I can get so caught up in the world's ideas of bigger and better with the world's definition of success that I manipulate my (future) husband and those around me to meet the standard of living I envision for myself. Or I can be a woman that is honorable, sacrificing, seeks to do God's will and puts the greater good before my own. Which woman have you chosen to be?

Regardless of what you may think about our First Lady, it is evident the type of woman that she is to her husband and her family. It is evident the type of woman she became and the type of woman that President Obama decided to marry.

If you are single, choose wisely in your mate. If you are married, it's never too late to change into the godly person God has called you to be in His image.

Reflection & Study Questions

**1. What are the key things that you are (single) or were (married) searching for in a your mate?**

**2. What are the deal breakers and things that must be maintained in order to sustain you in a relationship?**

**3. Are these things a reflection of Him and things that you are obtainable for your mate?**

**4. Are your standards too high that you frustrate yourself and your (potential if single) mate?**

Shaniqua Rischer

## In the Darkest Hour the SON Shines

*"At noon, darkness fell across the whole land until three o'clock. At about three o'clock, Jesus called out with a loud voice, "Eli, Eli, lema sabachthani?" which means "My God, my God, why have you abandoned me?"...Then Jesus shouted out again, and he released his spirit. At that moment the curtain in the sanctuary of the Temple was torn in two, from top to bottom. The earth shook, rocks split apart, and tombs opened. The bodies of many godly men and women who had died were raised from the dead. "Matthew 27:45-46, 50-52 NLT*

*"In the beginning was the Word, and the Word was with God, and the Word was God. He was in the beginning with God. All things were made through him, and without him was not anything made that was made. In him was life, and the life was the light of men. The light shines in the darkness, and the darkness has not overcome it." John 1:1-5 ESV*

This past month has been a struggle for me. My mind has been a war zone between faith and trust with fear and doubt. I am operating with my last financially and I have been trying do everything in my will by looking for jobs that will support me, <u>even though</u> I don't believe God is directing me to a conventional 9 to 5 job and beyond where He has me. Now before you misunderstand me, I am not saying God has told me to be a bum. Yet the more I try to do things in my will, the more doors have closed. I have been scared of falling flat on my face and losing everything I have including my home. I have wondered what shame I would feel if that was to come to past and what kind of glory God could get from that. I have wondered if I have been foolish. You see, I struggle with letting go and letting God. I am a fighter and a hustler (I have always been able to find a job and/or source of income through hard work and talent) yet the more I try, the more I feel as if I am spinning my wheels. This is a first for me. It's also been hard because I have been obedient. I am doing what God has assigned me to do. And guess what? I have wondered how can I be following God's will obediently, yet be facing this cliff. I wonder if Jesus asked the same question as He faced the cross.

But God has written me a love letter. He has written a love letter in my heart, in my mind, and in my Spirit. In that love letter, the most important thing He told me these past few days is that the Son shines in the darkest hour.

*The SON shines in the darkest hour.*

That's what He told me. Those were the very words whispered to my spirit and with those words; He took me to the cross. He took me to Jesus. It may look like all doors were closed on Good Friday. Jesus hung on a cross accused, beaten, and broken. Dead. Yet when death occurred, when everything looked to be over and done with, that is when the Son did His greatest work. In this scripture we see history at its darkest hour. We are witnesses to the hours of Jesus Christ's death. But as it is now a part of history that means we also know the resurrection came next. We know that the Son did His greatest work in the dark as He conquered death and sin once and for all.

*The Son shines and is LIGHT in the darkness.*

I am now thankful for closed doors. It's hard, I will not lie, but closed doors are forcing me to a new level of dependence on God. I know just what I can do and am capable of in my own hand. Yet do I know all that God is capable of? No. My mind cannot conceive all that He is capable of because my mind is finite and He is infinite.

**Reflection & Study Questions**

**1. What doors are closing in your life? Where are you at your last? Mentally? Spiritually? Financially?**

**2. Where do you feel that darkness is trying to crowd you and extinguish the light?**

**Whatever it may be, know that the love letter God gave to me wasn't just for me. The SON shines in the darkest hour and the LIGHT always wins. I rest in knowing that for my future. May you as well.**

Shaniqua Rischer

# Chapter 5: Encore: A Maturity Yet to Be Defined…The Trust Experiment

### The Trust Experiment

*"Trust in the LORD with all your heart, and lean not on your own understanding; In all your ways acknowledge Him, And He shall direct your paths." Proverbs 3:5-6 ESV*

*"Finally, brothers and sisters, whatever is true, whatever is noble, whatever is right, whatever is pure, whatever is lovely, whatever is admirable—if anything is excellent or praiseworthy—think about such things." Philippians 4:8 NIV*

*"God is not human, that he should lie, not a human being, that he should change his mind." Numbers 23:19 NIV*

I just did the unthinkable. Well, unthinkable to some. I just quit my job. I don't have an abundance of money saved up. I have no new job in the pipeline. But what I do have is God. The day before I quit my job, I was sitting at my desk and I got the overwhelming feeling of being stretched like taffy over and over and over again. So much so, I figured that would be the topic of my next devotional and found a picture online of a taffy machine to include. At that moment, I wondered when I would finally tear from the constant strain and stretching I had with my job. Who knew that today I would experience the tear? So family, what next?

As you can imagine, there are many things going through my mind. Fear. Peace. Wonderment. Fear. Yet just as my mind seems to be overcome with tumultuous thoughts, these three scriptures have come to mind.

"Trust in the Lord…" In this God is calling me to trust Him, just as I have several times before. The funny thing about trust is that it is always evolving. Just when you get to one level of trust, you are called to another one. God seeks to take you deeper.

"Whatever is true, whatever is right…think on such things". If I let my mind think about all of the negative things that could happen in this down economy, I would surely drive myself crazy. The mind is a powerful tool that the devil seeks to control, but instead of giving into fear, doubt, or anxiety we should walk by faith and focus on those things that are true, right, and admirable. We should think on these things of God.

"God is not a man…" How glad I am that God is not a man; instead He is the Promise Keeper. He is the only promise maker that keeps every promise. He does not lie and His word never returns unfulfilled. And the promise I am standing on, foolishly or faithfully – depending on whom you ask, is that I will not be forgotten or forsaken. He saw my sacrifice.

These are the words of God whispering to my spirit. I am not walking in the absence of fear; I am walking in spite of fear. I am moving. I am seeking and I am following Him.

This ministry, these devotionals, have always been my faith journey which I have openly shared; a journey of my struggles, my highs, and my lows in my walk with God. Today is no different. You see, what is about to happen in my life is the unknown. God is calling each of us deeper in trust with Him, deeper in relationship with Him. Can you sense it? It is easy to say that I have been foolish in my actions, but as of today my life has become the ultimate experiment in faith for your observation.

**Reflection & Study Questions**

**YOU now have full access to this experiment. Even before starting, I am sure of the outcome. To God be the GLORY. But for those who have doubted, who have wondered, who have struggled, who have lost. I welcome you to walk with me. God is always taking us places. Let's see where. Are you ready?**

Shaniqua Rischer

**Perfect Strangers**

*"The word of the LORD came to Jonah son of Amittai 'Go to the great city of Nineveh and preach against it, because its wickedness has come up before me.' But Jonah ran away from the LORD and headed for Tarshish. He went down to Joppa, where he found a ship bound for that port. After paying the fare, he went aboard and sailed for Tarshish to flee from the LORD. Then the LORD sent a great wind on the sea, and such a violent storm arose that the ship threatened to break up. All the sailors were afraid and each cried out to his own god. And they threw the cargo into the sea to lighten the ship. But Jonah had gone below deck, where he lay down and fell into a deep sleep. The captain went to him and said, "How can you sleep? Get up and call on your god! Maybe he will take notice of us so that we will not perish." Jonah 1:1-6 NIV*

Last week was Martin Luther King's birthday and no matter what your opinion of the man, it cannot be denied that he served as a catalyst for change in America. His obedience to his purpose affected the lives of many and helped change the course of a nation. That was Dr. King's obedience, yet what about yours? Have you ever given thought as to how your obedience or disobedience affects others? In our society, we are taught to believe that we are independent of each other; we believe our actions affects us largely, but at minimum our closest family and friends. If we are honest, we never think how our actions affect the lives of perfect strangers and if we do give thought to it, it is quickly dismissed or minimized. After all, how can our actions truly affect strangers or even the multitude? Yet scripture gives us a perfect example of how our solitary actions not only affect us, but affect those whom we have never met. Jonah received a Word from God and instead of obeying that Word, Jonah acted in disobedience and fled to a ship that would take him to Tarshish.

Soon after, a great storm raged, and the very ship Jonah used as an escape became a near death prison for he and all aboard. However, to me, the most interesting aspect of this biblical recounting is not that the storm was directly tied to Jonah's disobedience, what is interesting is how perfect strangers were in a bad situation because Jonah chose to flee. Perfect Strangers. We never know the effect of our actions on others; many times we view the ripple as having an immediate effect in our lives never realizing that the effect can be felt for years afterward. Someone once made a decision that affects you today. You may not know the person's name, but a decision was made. You too have made decisions that affect people you have never met.

As I near my last days at work, I have come to wonder what actions my leaving has set in place. I believe that God will protect all of the individuals I have ministered to, but it has crossed my mind as to whom will I not minister to because I have chosen to leave? It is a question I will never know the answer to. I pray for myself and for those perfect strangers anyway.

Eventually, after being thrown overboard from the ship, after staying in the belly of a great fish for three days, Jonah would submit to God's will and go to Nineveh and preach His word. From that delayed obedience an entire city would repent and receive the mercy of God's hand. They repented because of the Word that Jonah delivered. Our actions affect more than us, they always do. You don't have to hold a position of power or have the world as your stage to change the world for someone you may never meet. Instead, all you have to do is be obedient to where God is calling you to serve and how He is calling you. Begin to tell someone about Him or to finally walk out on faith and caste your cares on Him.

**Reflection & Study Questions**

**1. Have you ever given thought as to how your obedience or disobedience not only affects you, but can also others?**

**2. Where have you felt the impression or felt firsthand the cost of someone else's decision? What was the outcome?**

**3. How can you begin to make better choices and begin to affect the world in a positive way?**

Shaniqua Rischer

## All Things

*"And we know that all things work together for good to those who love God, to those who are the called according to His purpose." Romans 8:28 NIV*

*"And they said everyone to his fellow, "Come, and let us cast lots that we may know for whose cause this evil is upon us." So they cast lots, and the lot fell upon Jonah. Then said they unto him, "Tell us, we pray thee, for whose cause this evil is upon us: What is thine occupation? And from whence comest thou? What is thy country? And of what people art thou?" And he said unto them, "I am a Hebrew; and I fear the LORD, the God of Heaven, who hath made the sea and the dry land." Then were the men exceedingly afraid, and said unto him, "Why hast thou done this?" For the men knew that he fled from the presence of the LORD, because he had told them. Therefore they cried unto the LORD and said, "We beseech Thee, O LORD, we beseech Thee, let us not perish for this man's life, and lay not upon us innocent blood! For Thou, O LORD, hast done as it pleased Thee." So they took up Jonah and cast him forth into the sea, and the sea ceased from her raging. Then the men feared the LORD exceedingly, and offered a sacrifice unto the LORD and made vows." Jonah 1:7-16 KJV*

As I was writing the devotional, Perfect Strangers, I already knew what today's devotional would be. Does "it" really work for good? While in Bible College, I wrote a paper on the purpose of pain (made a "B" because I didn't use enough scripture reference) because I have always wondered how a loving God, could have create a world with so much hurt, pain, and anger. At times I still question that and admittingly, depending on the circumstance, I probably will again. However, as I have grown older, I now understand something. All things DO work for good. Even when we can't see it; they do. When Jonah disobeyed God and chose to flee to a ship, his disobedience endangered the lives of everyone. Due to the actions of one man a near tragedy occurred. Also due to the actions of that same man, many would come to know and praise God. Before the storm, the men on the ship knew many gods – all ineffective. During the storm however, they came to know THE One and only God. What would have happened had Jonah not gone to the ship? We will never know, but what we do know is that God used Jonah's disobedience to show His perfect power and perfect will to individuals who did not know of Him before. Working for good.

When I look at this life lesson, I couldn't help but look at my current and past situations. What good has come from my journey this past year? I have gotten the opportunity to pray for and help people. What good will come out of my leaving my job? Only God knows, but good comes. The good that comes from our trials may not always be recognizable or immediate, but God does use us to execute His will. His good and pleasing will. So where are you struggling to see the good in your circumstance? How has God used your hardships to bring you or others closer to Him? Not every bad thing is meant to harm us and not all bad things are meant to correct us. Sometimes, we experience things that are solely because of the actions of others. However, whatever the reason, God can redeem any situation for good. Anything.

**Reflection & Study Questions**

**1. As you review each second, day, hour, month and year of your life, what could you have done better?**

**2. What lesson or lessons did you learn from your experience?**

Shaniqua Rischer

**Get Out Of the Boat**

*"And Peter answered Him and said, Lord, if it is You, command me to come to You on the water. So He said, Come. And when Peter had come down out of the boat, he walked on the water to go to Jesus. But when he saw that the wind was boisterous, he was afraid; and beginning to sink he cried out, saying, Lord, save me! And immediately Jesus stretched out His hand and caught him, and said to him, O you of little faith, why did you doubt?"* Matthew 14:28-31 NKJV*

Today is the first day of my unemployment. Today! As I have been preparing for this mentally, it occurred to me that it doesn't really matter if I succeed or not to me; although I truly deep down do want success. What matters is that I tried. I tried to follow my dreams, I tried to give God my best, I tried to live my life by faith and I tried to get out the boat.

When Jesus told Peter to get out of the boat, He was giving Peter a glimpse of what His future could hold simply through faith. Jesus could walk on water; therefore Peter could too. So often we hear this story and marvel at Peter's fear and how it caused him to sink as he was walking on water after Jesus called Him. We foolishly think that it had been us that Jesus called we would have gotten out the boat and continued walking in absence of fear; after all it is Jesus that has called him. But what's so different about today than what occurred then. We are more powerful than Peter ever was. Yes, more! Christ told us that He would never leave us and He is certainly with us. More importantly for those that are Believers, we are indwelled with the Holy Spirit; the Spirit that Jesus, himself, said would allow us to do even greater miracles. But why don't we? Just as Jesus spoke to Peter to get out the boat, He has spoken to you as well. Jesus has invited you to walk on water as a matter of faith. So why aren't you? Your water may look different than mine, your boat moment may have occurred once, but that doesn't mean it won't occur again. Christ is always calling us to new levels of faith just as he did Peter. Before Peter's boat moment, he had witnessed the feeding of the five thousand. Before Peter's boat moment he had seen demons caste out, yet the more he walked with Jesus, the more Christ called him to a higher and deeper level of faith. He is calling you as well. The world we live in is not getting any better. It's not. Yet God is preparing soldiers to do great things in His son's name. Sacrificial things. Faithful things. He is calling each of us to get out the boat. It is now my turn. It is now your turn. It was easy for Peter to witness the miracles of Jesus in someone else's life, but it became harder when it was his own miracle he was called to participate in. Having the faith to walk on water is not easy, but it is doable.

Lastly, have you ever noticed that as Peter took the leap of faith to get out the boat and walk on water; the other disciples stayed put? Not one said "if Peter can do it, then I can too" and got out the boat to walk on water with Jesus too. Sometimes you have to be that one.

**Reflection & Study Questions**

**1. Are you a Peter too?**

**2. If not, what is keeping you from getting out the boat and walking on water? What is stopping you from joining Jesus on the "water".**

**My fellow Peters, I will see you on the water together as one.**

Shaniqua Rischer

## Good Enough

*"For You formed my inward parts; You covered me in my mother's womb. I will praise You, for I am fearfully and wonderfully made; Marvelous are Your works, and that my soul knows very well." Psalm 139:13-14 ESV*

Unlike many, I did not watch the full funeral of Whitney Houston. Instead I only saw five minutes of the funeral where Kevin Costner spoke about the friendship and common bond held between him and Whitney Houston. His speech was eloquent and left all with the very real understanding of Whitney Houston's humanity. The one thing that struck me repeatedly in his recollection of Ms. Houston was the self-doubt she faced as an actress, as an artist, and as a woman. Known as one of the greatest voices of the 21st century, listening to Kevin Costner and even Ms. Houston herself through interviews, you get the sense that her world was, at times, full of doubt. She wondered if she was "good enough". Good Enough.

As I heard those words, I was struck with how often I have thought those same things about myself and how I had heard similar thoughts expressed from family, friends, and even strangers. It would seem that the thing that ties humanity is in fact our humanity. The need to know that we are cute enough, good enough, fast enough, smart enough or just enough for whatever we measure ourselves by. We all have our "enough" moments and for some, those moments turn into ruling passions that push us to so called greatness and for others they cause us to constantly seek affirmation from people that seek to become the same thing we do, good enough.

At the end of Mr. Costner's speech, he made a statement that was so simple it was profound. He stated that now, standing before the Lord, Whitney Houston would finally recognize that she was "good enough".

The greatest lover, the Creator, would be able to affirm what Ms. Houston always sought, what I have sought and what you have sought; that we are good enough. Well, what so many of us fail to recognize is that we don't have to wait to stand before God to find that out. Instead, since the beginning of time, God has whispered to us that we are. You see we are good enough because God made us. Psalm 139 is one of the most beautiful passages of scripture because it shows us how we were created and accepted. God knew us in our mother's wombs (v. 13). He knew our failures; He knew our successes (v. 16); He knew our disappointments and yet Our Father, created us anyway (v. 3). There is no thought that we have that He is not aware of (v. 4) but He created us still. We are made in His image (Gen.1:27) and in that we are enough.  Oh, so much more than enough.


**Reflection & Study Questions**

**Whatever you struggle in or with; however you may find the enemy using your mind as a battlefield of doubt, know that you are more than enough. You are a marvelous work and skillfully made wonder (v. 15) of God. No one can take that from you, but only you can accept and embrace it. Are you ready to embrace it?**

Shaniqua Rischer

## The Promise

*"God is not a man, that He should lie; neither the son of man, that He should repent. Hath He said, and shall He not do it? Or hath He spoken, and shall He not make it good?" Numbers 23:19 KJV*

Have you ever had a promise from God that you thought would never come true? The scripture tell us that God is not a man that He should lie, but I must admit; at times I have wondered that if He isn't the liar, then perhaps I am. Perhaps I lied to myself to believe.

But…then I happen to think about Abraham and Sarah, when God told Abraham that he would be the father of many nations (Genesis 12:1-3). At the time, Abraham wasn't even a father and was well advanced into old age. In today's time, he and his wife, Sarah, would both be considered past child bearing days when Isaac was born. (Genesis 18:9-15, Genesis 21:1-7)

Or I think about Moses in the desert, wandering, wondering if his people would ever see the promise land. Having seen God deliver His people from slavery and seen the parting of the Red Sea, after wandering in the wilderness for almost 40 years surely it was a natural thing for Moses to doubt?!? But God had promised…(Exodus 6:1-8)

Or perhaps I think about the children or Israel and Judea, the Jewish nation, who for centuries believed that God would bring forth a great Messiah to save them. For centuries they waited on a promised to be fulfilled. (Psalm 110, Isaiah 9:6-7. Isaiah 53, Matthew 2)

Then I think of me. In 1999 in a little hotel room in Louisiana, one night God made a promise to me. Over 10 years later, I am just now seeing the first fruit of that promise. What does that say? What does Abraham, Moses, my story, and even the faithful promise to the Jews say about God?

It says that "God is not a man, that He should lie; neither the son of man, that He should repent. Hath He said, and shall He not do it? Or hath He spoken, and shall He not make it good?"

Throughout the past 12 years I have tried to erase the promise of God, tried to forget it, and convinced myself I lied to myself about it all in an effort to not believe it. Because believing at times meant I was to hope and to hope was painful. I am here to tell you now that God is not a man that He should lie. He simply is not. God does make promises and some promises may not be answered in 5 year or 10 years or even in our lifetime (as Abraham had no clue his seed would birth a nation), but He does deliver what He promises. Over hundreds of years, through enslavement, hardships, death and ridicule by others, the Jews were promised a Messiah until one day He was finally born.

God has promised you something and at this point in your journey, as you read this, you must decide what you believe about God. In spite of doubt, hardships, trials and tribulations, in spite of reaching your bottom or the number of years since you first heard His promise; you must decide what you will believe.

I write these devotionals as a person of Christian faith and I realize that not everyone believes as I do. I can simply attest to what I know to be true. Despite numerous witnesses, fulfilled prophecy, and personal testimonies of the life, death, and resurrection of Christ people still didn't believe. They still don't. Today, you have a choice of what to believe. Not just about Christ, but about that small thing God told you. That promise. Today it may not look as if the promise will ever be manifested; I am here to tell you that it WILL be. What God has promised WILL come to pass. This is not just my belief; it's my testimony, 13 years later.

**Reflection & Study Questions**

**1. What promises have you made to God and not kept?**

**2. Do you feel that since you have not fulfilled you promise that He will not fulfill any promises to you? Have you repented for not keeping this promise?**

**3. Do you believe He has forgiven you and have you forgive yourself?**

# Shaniqua Rischer

## Isaac Moment

*"And it came to pass after these things, that God tested Abraham and said unto him, "Abraham!" And he said, "Behold, here I am." And He said, "Take now thy son, thine only son Isaac whom thou lovest, and get thee into the land of Moriah, and offer him there for a burnt offering upon one of the mountains which I will tell thee of." And Abraham rose up early in the morning and saddled his ass, and took two of his young men with him and Isaac his son; and he cleaved the wood for the burnt offering, and rose up and went unto the place of which God had told him… Genesis 22:1-3 KJV*

"God is faithful. He sees your sacrifice…your obedience."

"His Will, will make that seem like chump change."

"…more blessings just unleashed because of your faithfulness."

All of these were texts my close friends sent me Friday after my Isaac moment. They were needed because after that moment, I had to recognize that I was either extremely foolish or extremely faithful. Before the decision was made, I knew that good things v. God-things always require a test. I had come to that epiphany a few days prior when I got the call. I never thought the test would be so hard. But it was.

What test am I talking about? Although I left my job, most would think my immediate thing to do would be to find a job. In part it is, but my focus within has actually been on ministry. I have started the beginning stages of developing my ministry, continue serving in ministry at church and continuing understanding different kinds ministry. Since then, I have interviewed for a few jobs, one of which ironically fell into my lap. I was called out the blue to re-interview for a job I had interviewed with few months back. Previously, it was between me and one other candidate. I had made it that close. When I got the phone call to see if I was still interested and asked to interview again, my spirit told me it wasn't for me. I made a date to interview. When they called me 3 days later to move the interview date, my spirit told me the job wasn't for me. When I interviewed, my spirit was shouting so loud that you would think I would then accept what I was being told and tell them never mind. You would think that I didn't. In spite of those God-moments where I ignored the spirit, I was focused on dollar signs more. This job would pay more than I had ever made and that's all I could focus on as I walked out 99.9% sure the job was mine. This was my test., just as Abraham had a test, the Isaac test.

Abraham was 100 years when Isaac was born (Genesis 21:5), the long awaited son God promised. Yet years later, after Abraham would nurture and raise his son, God would test Abraham with the very things he loved and always wanted, his son Isaac. The Bible recounts how the Patriarch of Judaism and Christianity would be tested through the ultimate sacrifice. God called Abraham to take his son to the land of Moriah and sacrifice his son as a burnt offering; to give up what was most important to him (his son) and act in obedience to what God told him to do. As Abraham took his son to that mountain, he went without hesitation (it didn't take 3 nudges of the Spirit) and he went fully prepared to sacrifice Isaac in the name of the Lord. The all-knowing God knew Abrahams thoughts. He knew that Abraham was prepared to kill and offer his son as a sacrifice. God knew Abraham's love, He knew Abraham's desire, but more importantly He knew Abraham's obedient heart. Because of that obedience, because of that willingness to sacrifice, God blessed Abraham abundantly. Abraham, the Father of Nations. (Genesis 22:16-18).

We've all heard the story before and know that instead of Isaac, God provided the ram for the sacrifice. Have you ever thought what you would do when you faced with your own Isaac moment? When God has called you to sacrifice something you hold dear to you, what will you do? Will you stumble and focus on the wrong thing like I did or will you move however He calls? What will you do when God calls you to sacrifice before you see the provision that is to follow?

Well, I wish I could tell you I acted as Abraham, but I didn't. It took me leaving that interview with a heavy spirit and a restless, peace-less evening before I finally listened to God's voice. The next morning I withdrew my name from the running so they could find a person who was not only passionate about their work, but whose purpose aligned with theirs. I was passionate about the mission, but I knew it wasn't my purpose. I knew that God has something different in store for me. I also wish I could tell you that I see my ram in the bush and that I've already seen the provision to my obedience. I have not, but I have faith that I will. All God-things require a test and I can only hope that even if I didn't make an "A" on my test, that I at least passed. That is my hope for you too. When you walk closer with God you come to understand that not all good things are God-things. Therefore, you have to be aware of those tests. Those are the moments that will present themselves and when you may be faced with the ultimate test to prove how much do you really trust God. It's not an easy test, but having already taken the class, I am prayerful that my notes have prepared you sufficiently.

**Reflection & Study Questions**

**1. Have you ever been faced with your own Isaac moment?**

**2. Has God has called you to sacrifice something you hold dear to you? How did you respond? Did you stumble and focus on the wrong thing as and many others have or will you move however He calls?**

**3. What do you fear?**

**4. What if (and when) God calls you to sacrifice before you see the provision that is to follow? Could you remain faithful and follow Him?**

# Living His Word

*"Thy testimonies are wonderful; therefore doth my soul keep them. The entering of Thy words giveth light; it giveth understanding unto the simple. I opened my mouth and panted, for I longed for Thy commandments." Psalm 119:129-131 KJV*

*"The righteousness of Thy testimonies is everlasting; give me understanding, and I shall live." Psalm 119:144 KJV*

Last week, after discussing with two of my friends about the job opportunity I withdrew from, they commented on the level of faith I had. It wasn't the first time I had heard such a thing and it probably will not be the last. I seem to find myself placed in situations where my walk turns into a testimony or example not only for others, but as a reminder to my future self. Yet my level of faith is not extraordinary. In fact, anyone can have it. We all can have faith to move mountains if we believe the word of God (and I do). But how do we get there? We study His Word.

Looking back on the past 10+ years of my life I have been in some form of in-depth Bible Study. In my early twenties, I was a part of an out–of-the box, game changing ministry called Spirit Groove where each week we meet in Bible Study, After Groove, to discuss and delve deeper into God's word. After that I enrolled in Bible College and let's just say the study of Theology will challenge even your most basic beliefs about God and cause you to delve deeper into His word in order to know Him. And for the last 5 years I have been a part of an International Bible Study that meets weekly. Throughout this time, I have encountered trials and tribulations, my faith has been tested and tried countless times, I have had joyful highs and experienced some "how am I going to make it out of this" lows. But I had His word to rely upon. Not the Word that my Pastor preached on Sunday, not the Word that my momma spoke over me as a child, but my own personal Word. Studying God's Word leads to living God's Word.

In Psalm 119 we encounter a psalmist who knew this very thing as well. One of the main themes throughout this Psalm is the desire to know God's law. Since the Psalm was written before the New Testament, the writer contends that in order to know God they must learn God's law, "Open Thou mine eyes, that I may behold wondrous things out of Thy law." (v.18) He was right. In order to know God for yourself you must know His word.

As I have grown older, I understand what Paul meant in Hebrews 5:12-14 when he speaks of the difference between the milk and meat of spiritual maturity. You have to be like the Psalmist and pant for God's word. You have to have a strong desire to know more, study more and as you do, God will reveal more to you and you can discern His will. You will walk in greater faith because you will come to know God's truth. *"Study to show thyself approved unto God, a workman who needeth not to be ashamed, rightly dividing the word of truth".* (2 Timothy 2:15 KJV)

My level of faith is not something that anyone cannot achieve. You too can walk away from any situation or temptation in the confidence of God. His word, the Bible, is an instruction manual, a shield, a double-edged sword, and a deliver. If you are seeking to grow in faith, you must seek to study His word diligently and not rely on your Pastor from the pulpit or your family and friends to show you God. I can only attest to how my life has changed with Bible Study. For years I have made a sacrifice of time to spend in Bible Study. A lot of people won't do that, but I encourage you to. If you want to know God on a deeper level, find a Bible study to join. Yes you can study alone (and you should), but there is a fellowship with studying with other believers who struggle too; other believers that pant to know His word also. It will be a sacrifice, but so was The Cross for you. I believe if we were to ask Jesus, He would say it was a worthy one.

**Reflection & Study Questions**

**1. What temptations or situations have caused you to walk away from God?**

**2. Have you spoken to Him about it?**

**3. Do you desire more from and or know that He desire more from you so you have walked about? Why?**

# Nothing Can Separate Us

*"Who shall separate us from the love of Christ? Shall tribulation, or distress, or persecution, or famine, or nakedness, or peril, or sword? As it is written: "For Thy sake we are killed all the day long; we are accounted as sheep for the slaughter." Nay, in all these things we are more than conquerors through Him that loved us. For I am persuaded that neither death, nor life, nor angels, nor principalities, nor powers, nor things present, nor things to come, nor height, nor depth, nor any other creature, shall be able to separate us from the love of God which is in Christ Jesus our Lord." Romans 8:35-39 KJV*

*"Jesus loves me this I know, because the Bible tells me so..."*

Do you remember that song? If only those words were easy to believe; unfortunately, as we said that as children we believed that it was as simple as that, but when you view your life through an adult lenses you see how naive children can be. Except for one thing the kids have it right.

Last week my Pastor used this scripture as the basis for His sermon "The Greatest Love of All" and as he delivered the sermon, I reflected on how I knew what I knew about God's love. Little did I know that Yesterday, I would be called to reflect again as I shared this very scripture with a friend who needed this reminder. My friend is struggling to find their way to talk to God because of how they feel their actions have separated them from God.

I wish I could say that the first time I knew God loved me was when I was a child, but it wasn't. Not really. Wish I could tell you that it occurred at the age of 25 when I was experiencing a life hardship, but it didn't. You see, I can't exactly point to you when I knew what I knew about the love of Christ, when that knowledge of His love became so rooted in me that it became unshakeable. I can tell you it was in my adult years after a series of trials and tribulations and triumphs. Because of those very experiences, I have come to live and breathe that scripture. Nothing separates me from the love of God through Christ Jesus. Not premarital sex, not adultery, not murder, not cheating on my taxes, not lying, not disappointing actions nor harsh words, not hell or high water, not the devil or strongholds and nothing can separate me from His love. Absolutely nothing.

Paul wrote the book of Romans as an introduction of Christian faith to believers. It would serve as a book of thoughtful explanations of what being a Christian means, how one becomes a Christian, and as a book of preparation for future Christians. This passage of scripture would be of comfort to those then and to us now.

Although there are consequences to our actions (I want to be clear that although we operate in grace and mercy, we also operate in consequences), God does not punish us because He does not love us. He corrects us because He does and He has to in order for us to the live the life He has prepared for us. Somebody today needs to hear and understand the depth and breadth of the love of God. Someone today needs to hear that over and over and over again. Someone needs to believe that and live that. Someone needs to know about the eternal and unconditional love of God. Someone needs to know about the power that is rooted in that love. God loves you so much that He gave His son for you. God loved me so much that His son died for me so that I could spend eternity with Him. As I reminded my friend of that, I felt the need to remind you. So many times we are hard on ourselves when we fail, that we stay down longer than we should. We walk away from the very love that forgives us and can heal us because we view God's love, sadly, through how we love. God's love isn't like that. Christ's love isn't like that. It's eternal. It's unconditional. It's powerful. We should never forget. God doesn't want us to.

**Reflection & Study Questions**

**There are consequences for not following God's instructions. God uses correction to grow us, teach us, and prune us. Know that He loves you and only wants what is best for you.**

**1. When God corrects you how do you feel?**

**2. Do you resist His correction or accept it?**

# Who Do You Say I Am?

*"When Jesus came to the region of Caesarea Philippi, he asked his disciples, "Who do people say the Son of Man is?" They replied, "Some say John the Baptist; others say Elijah; and still others, Jeremiah or one of the prophets." "But what about you?" he asked. "Who do you say I am?" Simon Peter answered, "You are the Messiah, the Son of the living God." Matthew 16:13-16 NIV*

*"He replied, "You of little faith, why are you so afraid?" Then he got up and rebuked the winds and the waves, and it was completely calm. The men were amazed and asked, "What kind of man is this? Even the winds and the waves obey him!" Matthew 8:26-27 NIV*

*"When he arrived at the other side in the region of the Gadarenes, two demon-possessed men coming from the tombs met him. They were so violent that no one could pass that way. "What do you want with us, Son of God?" they shouted. "Have you come here to torture us before the appointed time?" Matthew 8:28-29 NIV*

Yesterday I had lunch with a friend and he asked, "Why do we (Christians) even go to church?" I answered "Christ desires us to fellowship with other believers and that the church is a body of individuals working to fulfill His purpose". However, his question was more rhetorical as he expressed how we as Christian's text, talk, and even sleep (by the way, I have done ALL of the before mentioned, so I am talking to myself too) in church. He questioned if church has become just a Sunday "to do" item to be checked? Well, for me his question gave insight into a much deeper question: what do we believe and why? It is very easy to grow up in a Christian culture and automatically think you are Christian or even to practice Christianity without fully understanding basic doctrine, going through the motions without experiencing the Christ relationship or seeing a change manifested in your life. Without understanding exactly who Christ was, we will not have a true understanding of the reverence He deserves in church and outside of church. So, exactly who is Jesus?

There are numerous historical accountings that can support Jesus lived. The dispute has never been if Jesus lived or not. As a matter of fact, one of the common threads that ties Mormonism, Islam, Christianity and Judaism together IS the fact that we all believe Jesus lived. We all believe in Jesus.

But the greater difference is what we believe about Him. According to the Bible, Jesus commanded the winds and the sea; He caused demons to cry out, acknowledge His presence and submit in obedience; and He caused those who walked with Him to recognize that He was the Messiah they awaited. Those are just a few of the things said about Jesus. Yet, it is not only important to recognize what others said about Jesus, it is even more important to recognize who JESUS said He was: The Son of God. Jesus was more than a man; He was more than the mortal son of Joseph and Mary, however improbably a virgin birth may have seen to us. As I talk to various people of other faiths, I am not surprised to hear their beliefs and views of Jesus. Yet, do you know how many professed Christians believe that Jesus was just a Prophet? How many believe that there are other ways to the Father, other than through His son?

If we have basic confusion on that level, why would we hold His church (because it IS His) in reverence? If we place Jesus on our level, as just the Son of Man, then what is acceptable for us becomes acceptable for Him. For me, that is why it is so easy for people to text, talk, or sleep during church. Although I try not to text in church (if you see my phone, I am generally taking notes), I am guilty of talking to my friends at times and in my younger clubbing days, sleep did occur a few times (younger being the most important word there). Yet I find it harder and harder to do so now. I simply reverence Him so much. Christ was not only fully man, but He was fully God as well. He understood our struggles because He lived them, we DO have a friend in Jesus, but we also have a Savior in Him. A Savior that is God.

There are plenty of scriptures that can be used to support who Jesus is as the Son of God and the Messiah. The Book of Isaiah is full of prophecy that foretold of His coming. Yet my goal is not to prove who He was to you. Again, I write as someone that is a Christian. But, I do challenge you to find scripture that explains and supports what you believe about Christ. I pray that you identify scripture that will be planted in your heart so that you will no longer depend on what you heard about Jesus, but what you know.

Reflection & Study Questions

1. Who do you say Jesus was? List all of the reasons why you believe Christ is the Son of God and use scripture to support your claim.

As you grow in knowledge of His Sovereignty and Authority as the Living God, it becomes harder to give less than your best to Him.

Shaniqua Rischer

## Why He Did What He Did

*"For God so loved the world that he gave his one and only Son, that whoever believes in him shall not perish but have eternal life. For God did not send his Son into the world to condemn the world, but to save the world through him". John 3:16-17 NIV*

*"Father, the hour has come. Glorify your Son, that your Son may glorify you. For you granted him authority over all people that he might give eternal life to all those you have given him. Now this is eternal life: that they know you, the only true God, and Jesus Christ, whom you have sent. John 17:1-3 NIV*

I talk a lot. A whole lot, but as I have grown up, I realize I spend more time explaining than anything else. I am forever explaining my thoughts, my emotions, my actions and my words with the hope that I will be understood. You see (warning: explanation coming), I do not like confusion and lack of clarity so I often over compensate with people because I want to be clear.

This entire week, I have wondered how I would explain why Jesus' did what He did. I thought of all the Old Testament prophecies that spoke of His birth, death, ridicule, and debasement; I thought of the prophecies of His betrayal and being sold for silver. I thought for a bit. Then I thought some more. The only thing is, it's not about what I think. What would Jesus say about His own life purpose? How would He explain His death? Well, we don't have to wonder because although many times He spoke in parables, in this, He was perfectly clear. He did it for us.

He came that we would know God and the love of God; He came to complete the work His Father sent Him to do. Every breath He took was for us. He was born so that He would die for us. He died so that we would live eternally. Those thorns were thorns of love. The nails were nails of grace. There was no other way. All because He wanted us to have the same relationship with the Father that He did. He wanted us to be reconciled, unified, to our glorious selves in His image. Jesus came here with a specific purpose and job to accomplish and He was always on His Father's business. He was not apologetic about it and He dared to break barriers and push the limits in His ministry.

As I said earlier, I am guilty of explaining in the hope that whomever I am explaining "it" to will "get it". I am trying to convince them of my intentions or beliefs. It is an area that I struggle because on some level, I want acceptance and validation for what I am feeling or thinking. If I can get them to come to "my" way of thinking, then everything is good. Most of us explain for that very reason.

Jesus, however, did not explain His death for acceptance or even to convince others. He explained so we would know why the sacrifice was needed. He did not allow other's disbelief in His purpose to stop Him from fulfilling His purpose, walking in His purpose, nor being anointed in His purpose. that purpose was to serve God so fully, that all would come to know Him through His Son. No further explanation needed.

**Reflection & Study Questions**

**1. Do you believe that one of your life purposes is to serve God, so fully, that through you all would come to know His son?**

**2. If so, how can you fulfill this purpose?**

Shaniqua Rischer

## Every Man's Best Friend (Part I)

*"But he himself went a day's journey into the wilderness, and came and sat down under a broom tree. And he prayed that he might die, and said, 'It is enough! Now, Lord, take my life, for I am no better than my fathers!' Then as he lay and slept under a broom tree, suddenly an angel touched him, and said to him, 'Arise and eat.' Then he looked, and there by his head was a cake baked on coals, and a jar of water. So he ate and drank, and lay down again. And the angel of the Lord came back the second time, and touched him, and said, "Arise and eat, because the journey is too great for you." So he arose, and ate and drank; and he went in the strength of that food forty days and forty nights as far as Horeb, the mountain of God. And there he went into a cave, and spent the night in that place; and behold, the word of the Lord came to him, and He said to him, "What are you doing here, Elijah?" 1 Kings 19:4-9 NKJV*

In this scripture, we find Elijah at one of the most vulnerable points in his life. He had spent years doing the Lord's business. He was acting as a prophet because of the love, honor, and glory he had for the Lord. He stood against the prophets of Baal and stood for the love that God had for the children of Israel by proclaiming the Word of God. Yet, where did that obedience get him? Where did going the right way, the Godly way, lead? His decision led him to a place where there was a bounty on his head. Queen Jezebel sought to see him killed and in response, Elijah escaped death only to go into a place of hiding, praying for his own death.

For forty days, Elijah was so devastated, tired, crushed, and fearful that instead of walking in the ministry of the Lord, God sent angels to simply feed and minister to him. It is here that God spoke to Elijah. Have you ever been there? Like Elijah? Thinking that you were following God only to realize that you were walking into heartbreak or a place that you desperately wanted to flee? A place where you simply wanted the hurting to stop? I have.

I am every man's best friend. Literally. It is not something I aim to be or even start out trying to be, but invariably I am placed in the "best friend" position with all of my male friends. Now, before you feel some pity with that, I have had a pretty interesting group of male friends throughout the years and for the most part, I am extremely happy with being just a friend because I have witnessed them in their "relationships." However, I also believed the perfect place to find your mate is right in your own "backyard". That did not work for me; it backfired as a matter of fact.

The last time I fell for someone, it nearly crushed me and left me devastated to a point that I doubted myself as a woman and as a friend. The pain from that wound still haunts me at times as I try desperately not to repeat that mistake. Now I intentionally try a different approach when it comes to men. I am upfront, direct, and leave no room for confusion. Yet, in the end, I am in the same place I was the last time.

The last time I fell for someone, I lost my male best friend in the process because I simply fell in love with him. Our friendship was cultivated for more than a decade through laughter, shared experiences, hours of talking, and many times he was my shoulder to lean on. I adored him. But in the end, all he would ever see me as would be his friend. I realized I loved someone who would never love me the same as I did him. I felt betrayed by myself and by God. The very thing that I felt was of God (love) destroyed a relationship I cherished. As a result, my determination not to repeat history became my mantra, but here I am again - in the friend zone with no hope of moving beyond it. Although determined to treat my male/female friendships differently, I find myself here again asking why. Yet, before I can deal with the now, I must once again revisit the past and recognize the lessons I am missing, the strategy of the enemy, and where exactly it took me the last time.

Sometimes we think we are on the correct path, doing the things of the Lord and we come to a moment when we recognize that the ministry costs more than we have to give. The love we have for someone is not enough to keep that someone and circumstances leave you so bereft that all you want to do is throw in the towel. It is in these moments that God actually is preparing us to do His best work. In these moments, as we are hiding, God seeks to impart the vision He has for our future. Elijah was in the cave of doubt, loneliness, and fear, but he didn't stay there. God was about to call him out just as he did for me.

So, I left the cave I found myself in years ago and as hard as it was, I opened myself up again to someone that I grew to like. Once again, I find myself caring for someone who doesn't care for me. I took a different path this time and ironically, that path has led me right back to where I was before. Or has it???

Shaniqua Rischer

**Reflection & Study Questions**

1. Have you ever thought you were on the right path, but still something did not feel right?

2. If so, did you make an immediate change or did you stay on that path?

3. What did you gain or lose from this decision?

4. How can you prevent straying from the right path?

# Every Man's Best Friend (Part II)

*"The thief does not come except to steal, and to kill, and to destroy. I have come that they may have life, and that they may have it more abundantly." John 10:10 NKJV*

*"And the Lord said, 'Simon, Simon! Indeed, Satan has asked for you, that he may sift you as wheat. But I have prayed for you, that your faith should not fail; and when you have returned to Me, strengthen your brethren." Luke 22:31-32 NKJV*

This has been the most eye-opening seven day period of my life. It started last Friday with a conversation with a friend about my quasi-relationships with male friends. Quasi because although I have never been more than friends with those few friends I have liked, I understand that the relationships were mutually beneficial. I feed something in them by my attention to them and vice-versa; we become friends with emotional benefits. Two days later, my Pastor preached probably the most influential sermon of my life regarding the attacks of the enemy. It was not a "whooping and hollering" sermon and if I would have heard it 3 years ago, I probably would not have received it as I did. You see, with these past few years, I have been sifted as wheat AND was being pruned to grow at the same time. Sifted by the enemy and pruned by the Lord. Last Sunday the Word fell on fertile soil and that which was planted took no time in rooting and growing. I then questioned if I was repeating situations because God wanted me to learn a lesson or is the devil using his same strategy of attack on me over and over again? I believe it is BOTH.

The devil went to the Lord twice in the Bible to ask for permission to sift and test people, Job and Peter, and in both situations the Lord allowed it. But it wasn't until yesterday when I watched an online speech by Pastor A.R. Bernard that it became clear that in Peter's situation, Jesus prayed FOR Peter to withstand that test, not that He would deliver Him from the situation! My God! I have read that scripture repeatedly for years, but in the context of this past week it took on a whole new meaning. For years, I have repeated the same test and suffered the same attack of the enemy. Years! Each time the request was granted, Jesus prayed for me to withstand the attack. Jesus had faith in me that I would withstand time and time again, even when He knew my failures time and time again. Why? Because Jesus saw me in my glorious self. And He saw the Shaniqua that would not only finally figure out the enemy's strategy of attack, but would never succumb to that particular attack

191

again. Ladies and gentleman, I am that woman.

Going forward the devil is going to have to try a different attack. You see, the devil has attacked my finances before and that didn't stop my worship. The devil has attacked my body before as I lay on the floor crying in pain or the many times I could barely get out the bed because my hip and back was locked in pain, but I still kneeled and prayed through it. When the devil used my relationships with men and my heart as a weapon against me, I would stop praising, I found it harder to pray, and my worship wasn't as genuine. I found it harder to write devotionals or to minister to others. That one mode of attack always crippled me and affected my mind and my emotions. Each time doubt, fear, and low self-esteem would literally threaten to overtake me. I would spiral into a "woe is me" frame of mind and wonder why can't these men "see" me. I doubted me, I doubted my ability to be loved, and I doubted God's word to me. Time and time again, I would respond the exact same way until recently. This time, as I fell for someone that was a friend, I noticed two things. First, I honestly do not know why I liked this man, good and godly man that he is. With my former male best friend, I understood why I liked him. My feelings were based on years of interactions and him being a great friend to me - with this guy, not so much. We are friends, but there is no great friendship because we haven't built one as the tools we were using to build one are inadequate. I am honest about that. Secondly, I noticed that I was responding in the same way, however, as if there was a great friendship. When I was able to recognize those things, I saw the test, my lesson and the enemy's strategy.

Guess what? ALL of us at one point have had the EXACT same test. Yes, your circumstance and situation may be different, but we are taking the same test. God wants to grow us into spiritual maturity where our responses are different. Do we rely on Him? Do we complain in the test? Do we praise in spite of the test? Yet, as my Pastor pointed out, "Why would the enemy change his strategy if he beat you with it before?" If "Hail Mary" passes result in a touchdown every time, why do something differently? Let me tell you, the devil had been winning every time with me with the same play. Oh but, when you understand the enemies' playbook and you see how the enemy has used your weakness to gain a foothold, that play will never be successful again. That was the enemy's mistake with me. He used the same play on a changed woman. He didn't know the hours God and I have spent talking about my mistakes, he didn't know how I have prayed Psalm 139 over and over and over again, he didn't know how I was training off the field.

The devil comes to kill, steal, and destroy us as sheep. He wants to separate us from Christ so that we will be lost. We all know he has a strategy, but sometimes the issue is in recognizing how that strategy affects you. Jesus is standing with us on the field praying and encouraging us to stand, to learn, to go to the next level. I am every man's best friend and I am finally ok with that. It doesn't mean that those men don't "see" me. It means that they are seeing some of the best in me.

My prayer is to anyone reading this, please recognize how the enemy is seeking to kill you; destroy you; or steal what God has intended. Break whatever cycle or pattern you find yourself in so that you may live life more abundantly as Christ has ALWAYS intended.


**Reflection & Study Questions**

**1. Do you know what kind of life God had intended for you? Why or why not?**

**2. What cycles or patterns in your life do you need to break in order to live more abundantly as Christ has always intended you to live?**

## Shaniqua Rischer

### Birthday Cake

*"Therefore, if anyone is in Christ, he is a new creation; old things have passed away; behold, all things have become new." 2 Corinthians 5:17 NKJV*

*"He has saved us and called us to a holy life—not because of anything we have done but because of his own purpose and grace. This grace was given us in Christ Jesus before the beginning of time." 2 Timothy 1:9 NIV*

I like the song "Birthday Cake" by Rihanna. Actually, I more than like it…I love the song! I freely admit it, but I also feel guilty for liking the song as much as I do (if you've heard the song, you understand why) because the lyrics appeal to my old self. Since I have accepted my calling to preach, I am hyper conscious about my life and my walk as a Christian. Now, not only do I feel the pressure of being a Christian and not conforming to the world, there is something about being called to minister or preach that intensifies that feeling. So, as I am walking this journey, I have started to ask myself and God, "How exactly am I supposed to live holy?"

It's a question most Christians struggle with too. How are we supposed to live holy, being responsible for not only our walk, but careful not to cause someone else to stumble either? For years, I said "I am not Paul" when referencing some perceived Christian level of greatness. I said that to deflect my accepting my being called to preach, not realizing how that sentiment hindered my walk because I felt I could never be as "holy" as Paul. But you know what; Paul isn't me either (thankfully). Our Father created us both in His image and called us both to walk in our failures and strengths to bring Him glory and honor. The same goes for you as well. Some of my favorite people in the Bible were a murderer (Moses), a prostitute (Rahab), an adulterer (David), and not to mention the persecuting Saul aka Paul.

My point is that as Christians, we need to remember that the only Perfect Human was Christ, who was Perfectly God, and He died for our sins. We also need to remember that through Christ, we have been redeemed and are no longer the same people that we were before. Our strengths and our weaknesses now belong to God. All the doubt, insecurity, and mistakes, belong in the Savior's hands to be redeemed. We are a work in progress that will never be perfect on this side of Heaven, but are new creatures in Christ being shaped and molded daily in His image. Every person that did great things for God was a regular person with no great talents, but they made themselves available to God. That is the secret to being holy; being available and submitting ourselves to Him. By allowing God to use their (Moses, Rahab, David, and Paul) broken and imperfect selves, a new creature slowly emerged – not overnight. We become holy, we live holy, by opening ourselves to being filled by Him, submitting to Him, and being led by Him. In the beginning, it is not easy, but it is possible. Until one day, it becomes easier than you ever imagined.

**Reflection & Study Questions**

**1. Are you patient enough to wait on Him to change things in your life?**

**2. What have you asked Him to change or reveal to you?**

Shaniqua Rischer


## Who Are You Hiding From?

*"Then the man and his wife heard the sound of the Lord God as he was walking in the garden in the cool of the day, and they hid from the Lord God among the trees of the garden. But the Lord God called to the man, 'Where are you?' He answered, 'I heard you in the garden, and I was afraid because I was naked; so I hid." Genesis 3:8-10 NIV*

One of the most difficult things I have done is to learn to let my guard down. Even with my devotionals, it has been a concentrated effort on my part to let you into my life. Since my relationship with Christ has grown, I have learned to love people and open myself on a deeper level. It is still not easy. Like most people, past hurt and circumstances caused me to build walls I hoped would protect me. A part of that protection was hiding the true me for fear that I would not be accepted or loved, or that I would be found out to be a fraud, or to disappointment others. So I hid me. I protected me.

In the garden, Adam did the same thing, however because of different reasons. Adam was the apple off God's eye, made in His image, and given dominion over the world. Yet because of the craftiness of the enemy, he ate the fruit that was forbidden to him. And in that moment, he felt shame, he felt naked, and he felt fear of the very Lord who loved him dearly. Therefore he hid. Why? Because of what he now believed to be true, yet was in fact not true at all. If Adam would hide from God, who created him in His image and whose love formed him (Gen.1-26-27), it makes me wonder how many of us are hiding not just from God, but from others. How many of us are in hiding believing a lie about ourselves and not the truth of how God sees us or even how others see us? And what has that hiding actually cost us? It has cost us a life lived in fear of others finding out who we truly are, when who we truly are just happen to be people made in His image and formed in our mothers' wombs. (Psalm 139:13-14)

Fear and shame will make you feel naked and exposed, but I have learned that it is what we fear the most that actually has imprisoned us. The more open I have become with my failures and my faults, it is then the more love I have received. The need to protect yourself from exposure and shame did not start with you. It started in the garden, yet we have been hiding ever since. We hide, we lie, we shut down and shut out many with the hopes of protecting ourselves from being exposed and we fail to realize it is when we were the least covered, the most defenseless, that we received the greatest love.

I have a beautiful 4 month nephew and it saddens me to know the older he becomes, the more he will doubt the love that he has always had. He will eventually start to feel shame, to feel doubt, to wonder if he is good enough, smart enough, to fear and to hide all of the beauty and glory I see in him now. That God sees. But, those feelings don't always have to be there. I know because they are not that way for me anymore, at least not like they were. They don't have to be that way for you either. Stop hiding. Stop hiding from God and stop hiding from others. We can't hide from the greatest LOVER ever know, nor the love He wants others to give to us, and why would you want to?

**Reflection & Study Questions**

**1. Are you hiding from God?**

**2. Are you hiding from those who love you and want the best for you? Why?**

**No longer hide. Seek so He can show you that you can live gloriously and not in fear!**

# Chapter 6: Conclusion - My Voice, His Instrument…Oh! The Places You'll Go

**My Voice, His Instrument…Oh! The Places You'll Go**

*The word of the Lord came to me, saying, "Before I formed you in the womb I knew you, before you were born I set you apart; I appointed you as a prophet to the nations." "Alas, Sovereign Lord," I said, "I do not know how to speak; I am too young." But the Lord said to me, "Do not say, 'I am too young.' You must go to everyone I send you to and say whatever I command you. 8 Do not be afraid of them, for I am with you and will rescue you," declares the Lord. Jeremiah 1:4-8 NIV*

*"Congratulations! Today is your day. You're off to Great Places! You're off and away… Out there things can happen and frequently do to people as brainy and footsy as you. And when things start to happen, don't worry. Don't stew. Just go right along. You'll start happening too. Oh! The Places You'll Go! You'll be on your way up! You'll be seeing great sights! You'll join the high fliers who soar to high heights."* <u>Oh! The Places You'll Go</u> by Dr. Seuss

This year has been an incredible year for me. On my mission trip to Ghana, I found my voice. Actually it started a few years before, yet this year when I finally stepped out in faith and let God have complete and absolute control of my life, my voice emerged. In Ghana, I shared my testimony and presented workshops on self-esteem as a part of the Divine Women's Empowerment Conference. There my voice became His instrument.

When I was younger, I used to be loud. Everywhere I went people commented on how loud I was. I took note, but never really changed until my freshman year in college when I heard it from all of my new friends. Slowly one day, in an effort to fit in, I became quieter. But something ironic happened. Occasionally, people will ask me when I am talking, why am I whispering. I no longer even realize when I am speaking low. It is an unconscious, but learned response. That has also been the story of my life. Somewhere along the way, I have muted myself. I have muted the glory that God Himself breathed into me. My power, my beauty, my intelligence, and my strength; all things I have at one point in my life, down played. I am these things not by my own hand, but because of the hand of God. Yet for years, I acted and behaved less than I was. Are you doing the same?

In this scripture, Jeremiah attempted to act less than he was. He attempted to make an excuse for why he could not do nor be the person God created Him to be. There was only one problem. He was giving excuses to the one who created Him to be more. Are you behaving as Jeremiah and portraying yourself as being less than what you are?

I would know the answers in class, yet I would not answer them. I tend to remain quiet in group (outside of my close circle) conversations in order to not dominate the conversation and to diminish myself as well. I intentionally lessen myself so that others may stand out. Yet that is a disservice as I deny the God in me and I belittle the God in them. When I do this I am not allowing others to be better or allowing myself to grow. Yet that is what this ministry, the "Great Is" devotionals are about. "Great Is" is about the greatness of God; it is about showing my mistakes on my journey, but also challenging each of you on yours. Iron sharpens iron (Proverbs 27:17).

In Ghana, I finally found the last octave of my voice. But it was an experience that I never would have had if I did not allow God to be in control; if I did not finally believe I was exactly who God created me to be. Never again will I diminish myself because I recognize by doing so I diminish God. The same goes for each of you. God has whispered something to your spirit; a dream or a vision that He wants you to fulfill. And you may think you don't have what it takes, you may erroneously believe that you aren't good enough, but I say today that if you are made in His image (and you are), you are not only good enough, you are Great enough.

So, my fellow brothers and sister in Christ, if you would allow me to, I would like to share with you two valuable lessons I learned. First, "He's able!" More than you can imagine, God is able to do exceedingly abundantly above all you can ask or think (Eph. 3:20). The next would be "Oh, the places you'll go" when you let God have control of your life and your destiny. Jeremiah learned these lessons, may you as well.

### Reflection & Study Questions

**God wants you to live an authentic life, the life He has always envisioned for you. However, before you can do that you have to realize where and how you've lived your life less than what He has called you to live.**

**1. How can you live life authentic and abundantly?**

**2. Where is God asking you to trust Him in your life and recognize He is able? Do you believe that He is able?**

So what's the secret to an authentic life? The secret to an authentic life is a submitted life. You must give up everything of you, to receive everything of Him. Jesus wants ALL of you, not just the pieces you want to give Him.

Walk with Him…

Shaniqua Rischer

# ABOUT THE AUTHOR

*Passionate, Loving, Loyal, Engaging, Obedient, and Direct are* words often used to describe author Shaniqua Rischer. However, the words she loves to be known for the most are Christian and <u>daughter</u> of the Most High God.

Having struggled with low self-esteem, feelings of unworthiness and inadequacies, abject fear, and not knowing how to serve, love, and follow a God she could not see or feel made her tap into her inquisitive nature. Through intimate prayer and conversations with God, she gained a clearer understanding of the struggles many Christians face. The struggles include the responsibility of being called Christian; knowing what we are supposed to do, but too afraid to act or not knowing how to break free of the bondage that holds us captive. She has discovered a love un-like anything she has ever known, experienced favor that can only come from the Lord, and discovered what it means to finally let her guard down and let God be the center of her life.

In February 2011, Shaniqua began publishing weekly devotionals under <u>Greatls.org</u>. She is a member of Disciple Central Community Church where she serves as the mission's community leader and is in the minister-in-training program. Shaniqua holds a Bachelor of Arts Degree from The University of Texas at Austin and a Master of Arts Degree in Christian Education from Dallas Baptist University.

www.ingramcontent.com/pod-product-compliance
Lightning Source LLC
LaVergne TN
LVHW051630080426
835511LV00016B/2265